A Primer on Sustainability

A Primer on Sustainability

In the Business Environment

Ronald Whitfield and Jeanne McNett

A Primer on Sustainability: In the Business Environment
Copyright © Business Expert Press, LLC 2014.

First published in 2014 by
Business Expert Press, LLC
222 East 46th Street, New York, NY 10017
www.businessexpertpress.com

ISBN-13: 978-1-60649-634-3 (paperback)
ISBN-13: 978-1-60649-635-0 (e-book)

Business Expert Press Environmental and Social Sustainability for
Business Advantage Collection

Collection ISSN: 2327-333x (print)
Collection ISSN: 2327-3348 (electronic)

Cover and interior design by Exeter Premedia Services Private Ltd.
Chennai, India

First edition: 2014

10 9 8 7 6 5 4 3 2 1

Printed in the United States of America.

Abstract

What does sustainability in the business environment really mean? The concept has evolved from a vague goal to "save the planet" to become a strategic imperative for business to enhance performance across many dimensions. We live in an age of increasing corporate accountability and if a business expects to survive for the long term, it must adhere to ever higher standards of behavior and continuously develop more sustainable ways of doing business.

This book is dedicated to the understanding of sustainability in business by exploring the challenges of assessing and measuring it, by studying the systems thinking required to analyze it, and by developing a deeper appreciation for the ambiguity and complexity of improving it. The book provides concrete and practical methodologies and tools for implementation which are evaluated and discussed by means of debating sharply opposing points of view and by performing business case study analysis. Our approach encourages action. The book answers the question: "what can we do right now – in both our business and private lives - to improve the sustainability of our world?" A key characteristic is its comprehensive treatment of the complex issues sustainability raises for the business world.

This book is targeted primarily to business students and professors at the undergraduate and graduate level in all traditional subjects and in interdisciplinary courses

Keywords

sustainability, precautionary principle, corporate accountability, environmental movement, green washing, triple bottom line, sustainable business operations, sustainable innovation, sustainable supply chain, cradle-to-cradle design, life cycle assessment, corporate reporting systems, the global reporting initiative, the global compact, the carbon disclosure project, carbon footprint, water footprint, indices on sustainability, transparency, stakeholder theory

Contents

Preface

We want to share with you how we came to the conclusion that a book such as this one would be needed and what made us write it. We also want to explain its role in the Business Experts Press collection on sustainability and preview the book's organization.

A Primer on Sustainability takes a broad look at the ways in which the concept of sustainability is being applied in the business context. It answers the question, "What does Sustainability mean to the way we practice business?" A key characteristic is its comprehensive treatment of the complex issues sustainability raises for the business world. Our goal is to provide a concise, readable, introductory investigation of this far-reaching concept so that readers will have introductory access to the knowledge and skills needed to help their organizations understand and act upon the principles of sustainability. We also hope our readers gain a deeper understanding of the relationships between business, society, and the environment, and their critical role in these relationships.

When Ron Whitfield prepared to teach an introductory course on sustainability at the D'Amore-McKim School of Business at Northeastern University, he wanted the course, which addresses the complex issues sustainability raises for the business world, to provide students an introduction to the issues related to sustainability in the business context. He wanted a text that would assume no direct knowledge of the issues and at the same time, treat them in depth. He wanted to design a course that encourages interdisciplinary thinking. He also looked for student activities, such as debates and cases. Student activities are increasingly important as faculty and trainers seek to flip the classroom, or move from a directive and lecturing role to a facilitation role, with learners taking the lead in the classroom. Much to his surprise, there was no text to walk learners through the complex issues sustainability raises for businesses.

Ron established his course and tested materials and approaches in it, and then invited his Northeastern colleague Jeanne McNett to join him in the course and work with him to develop *A Primer on Sustainability*.

A Primer on Sustainability has also been written to function as the introduction to the Business Experts Press collection of books on sustainability. The following books will help readers build their in-depth knowledge in various areas of sustainability. Since Business Expert Press is committed to sharing knowledge in this growing field, you may want to visit their Environmental and Social Sustainability Collection to check for new resources at www.businessexpertpress.com/taxonomy/term/27/.

- *Sustainable Business: An Executive's Primer* by Nancy Landrum and Sandra Edwards
- *IT Sustainability for Business Advantage* by Brian Moore
- *Responsible Management: Understanding Human Nature, Ethics, and Sustainability* by Kemi Ogunyemi
- *Sustainability Delivered: Designing Socially and Environmentally Responsible Supply Chains* by Madeleine Pullman and Margaret Sauter
- *Sustainability Reporting: Managing for Wealth and Corporate Health* by Gwendolen B. White
- *Communication in Responsible Business: Strategies, Concepts and Cases* by Roger N. Conaway and Oliver Laasch
- *Developing Responsible Supply Chains to Drive Value: Management Insights, Issues, Concepts and Tools* by Robert Sroufe and Steven Melnyk

Our exploration in *A Primer on Sustainability* begins with an investigation of what sustainability means in a business context. Once the scope of the concept "sustainability" is established, we look at the systems and tools for sustainability. The second chapter explores ways to think about the process of sustainability (systems) and the assessment or measurement tools sustainability requires (ways to show the impact of actions). Systems include life cycle assessment and cradle-to-cradle design. Tools include corporate reporting systems, the Global Reporting Initiative, the Global Compact, the Carbon Disclosure Project, carbon footprinting, water footprinting, additional indices on sustainability, a focus on roles of transparency, stakeholder theory, and triple bottom line reporting, along with the analysis of sustainability offered by financial institutions.

We then move, in Chapter 3, to address critical issues in the area. The introduction of sustainability *in situ* is presented in a debate format, with both positions presented. The chapter also explores more deeply the critical issues in sustainability than previously. Next, we are ready for a direct application of sustainability concepts, in a series of case study reviews. These case reviews offer the learner further opportunity to explore the implications of sustainability in a business decision-making context. We review and summarize the challenge of each case but do not offer solutions. We recommend these cases for students to work on their own or for instructors and trainers to assign because we have found them most useful in providing learners further opportunity to think through some of the complex issues of sustainability.

The concluding section summarizes the major ideas introduced in *A Primer on Sustainability*. We propose three strategies moving forward: business needs to reformulate product and markets to become more sustainable; business needs to focus on more than simply profit; and government's role needs to be a positive force for change. We also want the reader to feel more comfortable with the level of complexity thinking about sustainability can require.

Acknowledgments

No book is ever produced without the encouragement, help, and support of many individuals. In this case, the ideas and content for this book grew out of a new course that was introduced to the students of Northeastern University in the 2010. In many ways, the first class was part of our experiment in how to teach the principles and practices of sustainability in the business environment to students of business. Some ideas worked; others needed to be reworked until we felt we had the right mix of theory, critical thinking topics, applications, and case studies. We received useful input from students along the way, and we are most grateful for this important feedback.

We have received generous and valuable support from our reviewers. We would like to thank Robert Sroufe and Chris Laszlo for their far-beyond what might be expected encouragement of our project. David Parker, the founder and president of Business Expert Press helped us develop the fundamental idea of a primer, Rob Zwettler provided us guidance once our project was underway, and Cindy Durant helped us with administrative issues. We want to acknowledge the help and support we received from everyone at Business Expert Press.

Our colleagues at the D'Amore-McKim School of Business at Northeastern University also supported us in this project. Colleen Pantalone helped launch the course at the undergraduate level, and Harry Lane, Marjorie Platt, and Harlan Platt helped launch the course at the graduate level, where the basic framework for this text was implemented. Harry Lane was instrumental in encouraging us to take on this project as a team. We received excellent research and technical support from Shawn Mullet, a former student and current colleague at Northeastern, and Pegah Karimi, a former student and post doctoral colleague. We also wish to thank Kathy Campbell, a strong believer in making the world more sustainable, for her generous financial support. We could not have completed this project without her assistance. Finally, we wish to thank our respective families for their continued support of our work on this project and all our professional efforts. To all these individuals, we offer our sincere appreciation for their support, constructive criticism, and many useful ideas.

CHAPTER 1

Sustainability: Meaning and Context

Learning Objectives

- Understand the various meanings of sustainability, including its relationships with nature and technology, applying a global point of view
- Differentiate between the concepts *sustainability*, *corporate social responsibility*, and *corporate accountability*
- Become familiar with sustainability as seen from a corporate perspective
- Grasp the concept of the supply chain and its importance to sustainability in the business context
- Become familiar with *A Primer*'s approach to sustainability

To begin our exploration of sustainability, we focus on its definition, an area that is a bit more complicated than we might think at first. We look at the supply chain, an important part of sustainability discussions, next and then move on to an exploration of sustainability's context. The chapter closes with a description of *A Primer*'s approach.

What Does Sustainability Mean?

Sustainability is a concept with no universally accepted meaning, and, as a result, it often means different things to different people. In this regard, it is similar to a concept in cinematography called the Rashomon effect. In the Japanese movie by the same name, four eyewitnesses to a single event tell their versions of what happened. Each witness offers substantially different but equally plausible detailed accounts of the same event. As director Akiro Kurosawa lets the story unfold, the film audience never knows for sure the true sequence of events. Students and scholars may have similar feelings about readings on sustainability.

Nature, Technology, and Global Considerations

Some experts believe that sustainability means that nature's bountiful resources (pure water, clean air, fertile soil) are finite and need to be protected. They distinguish between man-made capital (e.g., machinery and equipment) and natural capital—the resources that nature provides. One of their basic concerns is the question of how much we would pay for the creation of fertile farmland or other ecosystem services that nature provides for free. This perspective on sustainability builds upon the seminal work of Robert Costanza, Rudolf de Groot, and others. Costanza and his colleagues estimate that if we had to pay for ecosystem services such as pollination, soil formation, and over a dozen other services that nature provides at no cost, the value would exceed the global gross national product by a significant margin.[1] Of course, the monetization and estimation of ecosystem services will be a herculean effort that will depend on many assumptions and sophisticated models that produce a wide range of monetary values. Nevertheless, few doubt the fundamental conclusion that if we actually had to pay for ecosystem services, the global economic system would be quite different from what we witness today.

Man-made capital typically is owned and controlled by a single individual or corporation, but natural capital is generally a societal resource. Both forms of capital are valuable and both can be improved or degraded over time. When man-made capital degrades, we can fix it or replace it. When natural capital degrades, it can also be protected or improved, but this often requires collective or government action. For example, in the absence of regulation, cutting timber on public land results in the removal of more trees than can be replaced by normal replenishment and growth. Proponents of the protectionist view argue for putting a price on these resources because otherwise their value would be deemed insignificant. As a familiar business axiom states: "what gets measured, gets managed." If individuals and businesses acting in their own self-interest do not have to pay for the use of these resources, the resources will tend to be over-used. To cite another example, what if apple orchard owners had to pay beekeepers provide bees to pollinate their trees? Or what if the beekeepers had to pay the orchard owner to provide access to their apple tree blossoms so that their bees could make honey? We often take nature's resources for granted, especially if they are available to us at no cost. The challenge in developing measures of these services in monetary terms is dealt with by many authors including David Pearce in his book, *Blueprint for a Green Economy.*

Another group of experts focuses on the strong role that advanced technology and science can play in identifying and implementing solutions to our environmental problems. For every problem, they seek and expect to find a solution. These experts believe that there are technical fixes to all of the planet's ills and that they should be developed and implemented as widely as possible. For example, if chlorofluorocarbons (CFCs) that are used in refrigeration deplete the ozone layer, then science can create new chemical compounds that do not deplete the ozone layer. These new refrigerants actually have been developed. Similarly, if burning fossil fuels results in ever increasing levels of carbon dioxide and higher planetary temperatures, then action is required to find a variety of technological solutions to the problem—ranging from altering the volume of solar radiation that reaches the earth (giant mirrors in space) to storing large amounts of carbon dioxide in underground geologic formations (carbon sequestration), to promoting greater use of nuclear power. With the exception of nuclear power, these new technologies, often called geo-engineering, have not yet been developed.

The introduction of new technologies can create their own sets of issues, because there may be unintended consequences that follow from their implementation. As technology experts Michael and Joyce Huesemann argue, "… technology will necessarily produce both positive and negative effects. This character of technology creates a serious intellectual challenge for technological optimists who exclusively focus on the positive aspects of technology while ignoring the, often enormous, negatives."[2]

CFCs are a good case in point. Until they were invented, household refrigerators used toxic and flammable gases like ammonia as coolants. Small leaks sometimes resulted in explosions, fires, damage to property, and even death. Refrigerators were often placed in separate rooms or outdoors to mitigate these dangers. CFCs are colorless, odorless, nonflammable, noncorrosive, and nontoxic products that eliminated the danger posed by refrigerator leaks. In just a few years, refrigerators using CFCs

became the standard for home kitchens and later for commercial refrigeration and automobile air-conditioning systems. It was not until the 1970s
that scientists discovered the damage CFCs caused to the stratospheric
ozone layer, an unintended consequence of their use. CFCs have now
been replaced by more advanced products that do not damage the ozone
layer.

When faced with these scientific and technological uncertainties,
some experts prefer a "go slow" approach called the precautionary principle. Advocates of this principle deem it better to enact precautionary policies even before scientific consensus emerges, particularly in cases where
the use of novel technologies may have substantial, irreversible, or even
catastrophic consequences. An important milestone in the evolution of
this concept was reached at the United Nations Conference on Environment and Development in Rio de Janeiro in 1992 (often referred to as the
Earth Summit), when the participants endorsed Article 15, which states:

> In order to protect the environment, the precautionary approach
> shall be widely applied by States according to their capabilities.
> When there are threats of serious or irreversible damage, lack of
> full scientific certainty shall not be used as a reason for postponing
> cost-effective measures to prevent environmental degradation.[3]

In these cases, following this principle would avoid or at least mitigate
the potential damage that these technologies could cause to human health
and the environment. The precautionary principle is largely unconcerned
with balancing the perceived economic benefits of the technology against
its costs, an approach that is the primary basis of the regulatory system of
the United States and many other nations. Because science and scientists
have difficulty in quantifying risk or characterizing uncertainty, the precautionary principle generally favors status quo and tilts the playing field
toward falsely rejecting potentially beneficial technology, as opposed to
falsely accepting harmful technology. It has also been criticized because
the burden of proof that a technology is safe (as opposed to proving that
it does not cause harm) is borne by the technology's advocates.

Still another group of experts looks at sustainability issues from a
global perspective. Issues related to sustainability—like climate change,

water scarcity, and poverty—often require not only a global perspective but also global decision-making capacity. These experts often point out the divergence between rich, developed countries and poorer, developing countries. They often cite cultural differences, income inequality, and ecological footprints as factors to consider in comparative studies across regions. Many of these experts point out the need for global agreements on particular topics, like the Kyoto Protocols on Climate Change, with enforcement mechanisms to achieve particular goals. Many industrialized economies signed this agreement in the late 1990s, although the United States and Australia declined, and Canada withdrew from the agreement in 2011, citing the high economic cost of complying with the terms of the treaty. Global sustainability issues pose particularly difficult questions. How do countries prioritize their sustainability goals relative to their other goals, such as feeding the population, fostering rapid economic growth, and alleviating poverty? Second, is the imposition of Western-style environmentalism on developing countries entirely justified? Some experts claim that a rapidly growing emerging economy has different priorities, of which sustainability is only one of many. Other experts claim that the over-consumptive practices of the developed world may be depriving the developing world of the fruits of modern society.

Sustainability, Corporate Social Responsibility, and Corporate Accountability

These concepts of sustainability that we have reviewed here are closely related yet different from other movements with similar goals, such as corporate social responsibility (CSR) and corporate accountability (CA). CSR refers to voluntary business activities that account for the social and environmental impact created by the business. As currently practiced, this means that companies commit to develop policies that integrate socially responsible practices into normal business operations and to report progress on an annual basis to stakeholders. Early CSR reports often focused on philanthropy as a driver of CSR; for example, building schools in impoverished areas where the company operated. More recently, this concept has been supplanted by a broad commitment to protect and improve the lives of workers and the communities in which companies do business. Published CSR reports now routinely address issues impacting virtually every area of operations: corporate governance, worker hiring and training, relationships with suppliers and purchasing behavior, and the company's energy and environmental impact. Exhibit 1.1 compares the CSR approach with the concept of sustainability.

CA, on the other hand, can be "defined as the ability of those affected by a corporation to control that corporation's operations." [4] Under this strict definition, companies would be held to a much higher standard of behavior. In place of voluntary activities to improve a company's social and environmental performance, CA adherents propose the creation of institutional mechanisms that hold corporations legally responsible for their behavior on social, ethical, and environmental dimensions. These mechanisms would impose duties on publicly traded companies, their senior management, and the board of directors with respect to the company's performance and social and environmental impacts. Under the CA concept, legal liability would attach to corporate breaches of international laws and agreements, and enforcement mechanisms could be imposed.

There are some common grounds in these different viewpoints of sustainability, CSR, and CA—a concern to preserve the planet's natural resources and to implement a set of governmental, corporate, and individual policies and practices that reduces our carbon footprint and waste while conserving our finite resources. Similarly, as discussed previously,

Exhibit 1.1. Comparison of Sustainability and CSR Approach

	Sustainability	Corporate social responsibility
Value proposition	Firm creates socioeconomic benefits with a low environmental footprint—the company and community coming together	Firm acts as a good corporate citizen through philanthropy
Methods	Actions are integral to competition and long-term profit maximization	Actions are discretionary or because of external pressure
Strategies	Agenda is company-specific and internally generated	Agenda is determined by noncore business interests
Impact	Large impact because its actions realign the entire company budget and operations	Limited impact because its actions are intended to improve company image with few operational changes
Examples	Patagonia, Burt's Bees	British Petroleum

there are common grounds in the different perspectives about respect for nature, the role of technology, and the global aspect of the concept. Given these diverse perspectives, is it any wonder that the definition of sustainability has elicited such a heated discussion? The United Nations World Commission on Environment and Development, known as the Brundtland Commission, crafted the most widely accepted definition of sustainability in its discussion of sustainable development: sustainable development "meets the needs of the present without compromising the ability of future generations to meet their needs."[5] This definition requires balancing economic prosperity with environmental responsibility and social justice, and it is the one we use. Such an understanding of sustainability has implications for how we design, produce, distribute, and consume goods and services; how we establish market prices for these goods and services; how we provide and consume energy; how we respect and regulate the environment; and how we ensure health and well-being for all living creatures. Sustainability requires unique approaches to management of governmental institutions, markets, business organizations, and our own personal behavior.

Sustainability from a Corporate Perspective

The purpose of this book is to introduce readers to the concept of sustainability with particular attention to the ways in which this concept affects corporate strategy, public policy, and individual decision making. Our goal is to give readers the knowledge and skills to help them understand and act upon the principles of sustainability, and to gain a deeper understanding of the relationships among business, society, and the environment.

In this book, we examine a variety of environmental problems, including depletion of natural resources such as water and petroleum, global warming, the integrity of the food supply chain, and use and disposal of toxic substances. Many of these problems arise because of failures in the free market system: failure to account for externalities (costs imposed on others involuntarily), failure to fully understand the science, or failure to balance long-term costs against short-term benefits. Companies face these problems on a regular basis. Here are some noted examples:

- **Freeport-McMoRan's copper, gold, and silver extraction activities in Indonesia.** This is an example of a failure to account for externalities. Freeport-McMoRan operates the Grasberg mine, the largest gold mine and the third largest copper mine in the world, in the Papua province of Indonesia. Mine operations have generated a significant controversy because of the waste disposal methods and their impact on a sensitive ecosystem. The mine produces vast amounts of mine waste including some that are hazardous. Much of this material ends up in the nearby rivers as they flow out to sea. Although the company claims that the mine meets existing environmental standards for the area, others contend that the mine is causing major environmental damage. In addition to the environmental impact of the mine, the company has been held accountable for the displacement of indigenous people, criticized for the low percentage of profits shared with the local residents, and accused of corruption and lack of transparency about its actions. The cost of these externalities is not reflected in the exported price of the copper, gold, and silver.

- **DuPont's delayed acceptance that CFCs were destroying the stratospheric ozone layer.** This is an example of a failure to understand the science and the unintended economic and environmental consequences of ozone depletion. CFCs are a group of highly engineered chemical compounds used in applications like air conditioning and refrigeration equipment. They are chemically stable, low in toxicity, and nonflammable. After decades of commercial success, research chemists linked CFCs with ozone depletion in the early 1970s. DuPont disputed the finding and did not aggressively search for alternative products. Only after the finding was confirmed did the company accept the ultimate phase down of the business and ramp up the production of alternatives.

- **Dow Corning's breast implant business.** This is an example of a failure to understand scientific evidence of the health risks for women. Dow Corning's breast implant business contributed only 1% to its annual revenues of $2 billion in the early 1990s, but the corporation's inability to accurately assess the risks of this business and to take appropriate action in a timely manner led the company into a costly bankruptcy in 1995. Despite the early warning signals of trouble, it decided to continue manufacturing this product without adequately informing patients of the risks. This decision eventually resulted in over 10,000 lawsuits, many billions of dollars in legal costs and judgments, and serious damage to the company's reputation.

- **McDonald's discovery that it was contributing to rain forest destruction in Brazil.** This is an example of a failure to account for externalities not by the company itself, but by an important supply chain partner. In 2006, McDonald's created a working group to develop a more sustainable supply chain for its sprawling, global food requirements. A supply chain of this size has two major characteristics: significant purchasing power and immense complexity. For example, Europe restricts imports of genetically modified (GM) foodstuffs like soybeans and McDonald's needed reliable suppliers of non-GM soybeans for their Chicken McNuggets. (Note: Soybeans are used as a major ingredient in chicken feed.) Because over 90% of the U.S. soybean crop is genetically modified, major McDonald's suppliers such as Cargill, needed to look elsewhere for large quantities of non-GM soybeans. Cargill purchased its non-GM soybeans from recently deforested Amazon land in Brazil. Rather than targeting Cargill, environmental activist groups like Greenpeace boycotted McDonald's restaurants in Europe to bring public pressure for change. This action resulted in McDonald's digging deeper into the practices of its supply chain partners and initiating remedial actions.

- **Ford Fiesta's decision not to introduce a diesel-powered car in the North American market.** This is an example of the failure to balance long-term benefits against short-term costs. The Ford Motor Company launched the Fiesta Diesel car in Europe in 2008. The car achieved a rating of 65 miles per gallon, one of the most fuel-efficient vehicles in mass production in the world, surpassing even the popular Toyota Prius. It quickly became the best selling Ford model in the European market. Yet Ford decided to keep the technology out of the U.S. market, contending that it would be too expensive to export it to North America and that U.S. consumer demand for diesel-powered cars was too uncertain. It remains to be seen whether Ford lost an opportunity to capitalize on this technology in the North American automotive market.

"Yes, the planet got destroyed. But for a beautiful moment in time we created a lot of value for shareholders."

There are a number of ways to address these decisions related to sustainability, from a corporate as well as from a public policy perspective. Some analysts suggest increased government regulation as a solution for these market failures. Such regulation could take at least three different forms. First, the government could set standards, mandates, or codes to encourage the desired outcome. For example, in an effort to reduce the nation's dependence on imported crude oil, the government created a complex set of Corporate Average Fuel Economy (CAFE) targets that are intended to increase fuel efficiency and thereby reduce petroleum consumption. These regulations are imposed on manufacturers. Second, the government could impose a tax on consumers to achieve the same outcome. Such a tax on market activities that generate negative externalities is often called a Pigovian tax (named after the economist Arthur Pigou). When a market activity generates negative externalities, the social costs are not recognized by the private sector, and the market outcome is not efficient. In such cases, society will tend to over-consume the product. The tax is intended to correct the market outcome. Referring to the CAFE example cited earlier, the government could have imposed significantly higher gasoline taxes that would have achieved the same reduction in petroleum consumption (albeit with a different mix of automobiles on the road). Third, the government could impose severe restrictions or even an outright ban on the use of a product. Examples of partial or complete product bans include the pesticide DDT, leaded gasoline, and the artificial sweetener cyclamate.

Other analysts have proposed market-based solutions for market failures. In some cases (we explore some of these in subsequent chapters), entrepreneurs can identify market failures and underserved populations and create new businesses that address these market needs, in the absence of government subsidies or support. In other cases, business managers can identify sustainability issues in their individual organizations and provide a variety of innovative solutions. We examine some of the ways by which companies reduce their impact on the environment. Using a combination of readings, debates, and case analyses, we assess how both *government regulations*, such as taxes, subsidies, building codes, and prohibitions of use, and *business solutions*, including zero emissions, green design, producer take-back, life cycle assessment, and corporate environmental reporting, address these problems. We learn how some companies are acting decisively to become more sustainable, and how they are winning in the competitive marketplace. We learn how other companies are moving slowly and struggling with the day-to-day implementation issues. We also discover that there are other companies that make false claims of their sustainability accomplishments, a behavior pattern called "green-washing." Finally, since the general population is the ultimate consumer of the products and services produced by these businesses, we also address how individual decision making can play a catalytic role in the reduction of these problems.

Sustainability and the Supply Chain

Sustainability involves a new way of thinking about value creation. For example, it requires a new way of measuring the impact of our decisions and actions. In one traditional approach to measurement, the area of accounting, we measure the economic impact of business decisions, and not their social and environmental impacts. Historically, we have tended to see the impact of our business activities as disconnected from their contexts. Sustainability suggests that we think about our activities in a larger way, as part of a complex system of relationships. This means changing how we think, how we organize, and how we measure success.

In the early days of the sustainability movement, companies looked primarily at their own operations and measured their environmental and societal performance gains in a narrow way: how much less energy, water, and other resources their factories consumed that year compared with past years. In other words, they drew a circle around their physical assets and sought to optimize performance within the circle. Nowadays, companies realize that it is the entire supply chain that needs to be improved as they address their sustainability issues—direct suppliers (and the companies who supply the suppliers), the distributors, even customers who may wish to dispose of products that are no longer useful. In this book, we define a company's supply chain as all those activities that transform natural resources, raw materials, and components into finished products that are delivered to the ultimate customer. The circle has been enlarged to include the entire supply chain, from raw materials extraction, through manufacturing and use, to ultimate disposal.

Here are examples of narrow and wide supply chains found in municipal water operations. Most large municipal water utilities use chlorine gas to disinfect their drinking water, which they receive in bulk shipments by rail or truck. This supply chain is depicted in Exhibit 1.2.

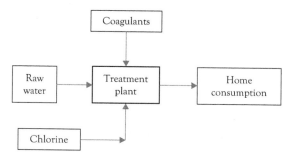

Exhibit 1.2. Narrow Supply Chain Example.

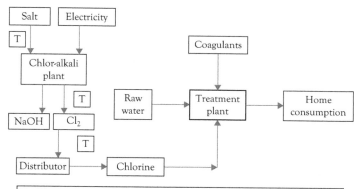

Exhibit 1.3. Wide Supply Chain Example.

If we look at this supply chain in a broader context (Exhibit 1.3), the plant that produces the chlorine gas for the water utility uses an electrolytic process to separate salty water into chlorine, sodium hydroxide, and hydrogen (a by-product). The salt is often supplied from a salt mine, while the electric power is provided by the local power plant. The electric grid uses a mixture of fuels that could include coal, natural gas, hydropower, or nuclear power.

Walmart offers another example of the supply chain's centrality to sustainability. Walmart is a company that historically has been heavily criticized for its environmental, societal, and labor practices. It has been inundated with the results of poor public relations, protests, and lawsuits, and typically it dealt with these issues defensively rather than proactively.

However, beginning in 2005, Walmart began to realize that making a profit by selling goods at everyday low prices and building a sustainable business were not mutually exclusive activities. As a senior manager of Walmart stated, "We recognized early on that we had to look at the entire value chain. If we focused on just our own operations, we would have limited ourselves to 10 percent of our effect on the environment and, quite frankly, eliminated 90 percent of the opportunity that's out there."[6,7] This is one example among many possibilities of how a company noted for its aggressively low pricing policy is doing good and doing well. As one leading expert states, "Supply chains are increasingly seen as strategic assets, and companies are placing greater emphasis on collaboration with suppliers and customers that are part of their 'business ecosystem'."[8]

The Context of Sustainability

Now that we have looked at the meaning of sustainability from multiple perspectives and examined the supply chain, we can make some generalizations about the context of sustainability. One of the most notable characteristics of sustainability and one of its most challenging is that its scope is likely to be at once global and local. For example, climate change effects are felt locally and individual actions to reduce greenhouse gas emissions occur at a local level, but the process of climate change cannot be addressed in a fragmented way; global cooperation will be required.

Managing any process in a global context is an increasingly difficult challenge because the global context is changing constantly and is increasingly complex. Scholars of global management have described this increased complexity in terms of four attributes: multiplicity, ambiguity, interdependence, and flux.[9] Multiplicity describes the increasing number of players or stakeholders involved in any one issue, whereas interdependence describes the increased levels of interconnectedness among these players. Ambiguity describes the increasing difficulty to give accurate meaning to information and is due to lack of clarity, confusion about cause and effect relationships, and equivocality or multiple interpretations of the same facts. We already have seen aspects of this complexity around the definition of sustainability. A close examination of many local efforts to introduce sustainability in the area of energy will yield additional examples of multiplicity, interdependence, and ambiguity. These attributes contribute, in turn, to the final attribute of the global context, flux. In short, everything in the global context is constantly changing at an increasing rate.

Our Approach

Given this increasingly complex and constantly changing environment in which issues of sustainability exist, our goal here with *A Primer* is to open these complex issues to a deeper understanding, rather than to lead to specific answers. We take this approach because in such a fluctuating environment, any specific answers may become dated before they reach the reader. If *A Primer* can convey an introduction to the process of approaching these issues, the reader will be able to apply this approach going forward. Our method includes exploration of the issues and their discussion. We are convinced that, through an understanding of these processes, we build our ability to grapple with their complexity and to influence the many issues related to sustainability that we encounter. Thus, our approach encourages action. It involves research, debate, case studies, and projects. Our belief is that through such active engagement, we will be able to meet our needs now "without compromising the ability of future generations to meet their needs."[10]

The ideas in *A Primer* are a synthesis of ideas drawn from the work of scholars and scientists. We want to be up front about this point: We are standing on the shoulders of giants as we pull together ideas that contribute to the fundamental concepts of sustainability in the business arena.

A Primer on Sustainability provides introductions to the areas of sustainability relevant to the business context. Chapter 1 has reviewed definitions of sustainability, placed the concept in a context, and outlined *A Primer's* general approach. Chapter 2 examines the systems we have for thinking about sustainability and the tools available to us to assess and measure it. Chapter 3 addresses the complexity sustainability presents and provides an in-depth exploration of seven major issues in sustainability. We include these explorations because we need to understand that the challenges of sustainability are not easy, yet they need to be sorted out and understood. Let's be up front and honest: If sustainability were easy to

Exhibit 1.4. Summary of A Primer's *Basic Concerns and Pedagogical Aspects*

Chapter	Basic concern	Pedagogical function
Chapter 1 Sustainability: Meaning and Context	How can we understand sustainability in a business context?	Introduces the topic and terminology
Chapter 2 Systems and Tools for Sustainability	How can we think about, measure, and compare sustainability?	Introduces conceptual and analytical approaches to sustainability and its measurement
Chapter 3 Thinking About Major Sustainability Topics	What are some of the major issues and how can they be addressed?	Offers a model for analysis of complex sustainability issues
Chapter 4 Decision Making in Sustainability: Case Studies	What sorts of decisions related to sustainability do businesses face, and around what issues?	Offers application potential
Chapter 5 Concluding Thoughts	What can we do right now and in the future? How does our commitment to sustainability affect the way we conduct our business and private lives?	Summary and review of commitment to engagement with sustainability

attain, we would already be there. Who doesn't want to leave succeeding generations with the same tremendous natural resources to which we have been given stewardship? Chapter 4 continues this exploration of sustainability's complexity with reviews of recommended case studies that cover sustainability in the business context. Chapter 5 summarizes *A Primer* and looks to the future. Exhibit 1.4 summarizes our approach.

CHAPTER 2

Systems and Tools for Sustainability

Learning Objectives

- Build knowledge about the conceptual systems that help us understand sustainability processes
- Review the methodology for life cycle assessment and its application
- Become familiar with cradle to cradle design
- Understand the challenges of assessing and measuring sustainability
- Become familiar with the major corporate sustainability reporting systems and their uses—the Global Reporting Initiative, the Global Compact, the Carbon Disclosure Project, carbon footprinting, and water footprinting
- Become aware of the other UN indexes such as the Human Development Index and the Human Sustainability Index
- Build awareness of ways organizations show their transparency on sustainability issues, such as triple bottom line reporting
- Review ways financial institutions evaluate corporate sustainability, including the FTSE KLD 400 Social Index, the Dow Jones Sustainability Indexes, and SAM

This chapter looks at the nuts and bolts of sustainability, ways to think about the process of sustainability and to measure the impact of our sustainability efforts. First we consider the systems that have been developed to help us think about sustainability, including life cycle assessment and cradle to cradle design. Then we move on to the tools for sustainability, which help us assess and share the success of our actions related to sustainability and the effect they have had. These tools include the

Global Reporting Initiative, the Global Compact, the Carbon Disclosure Project, carbon and water footprinting, various United Nations indexes on sustainability, triple bottom line reporting, and the evaluation of sustainability that financial institutions have done, which has led to indexed funds.

Systems for Sustainability

The ways to think about sustainability are a critical consideration as businesses begin to implement sustainability into the many processes in which they participate. Life cycle assessment and cradle to cradle design are two of the most accepted constructs that have been developed to think about the process of sustainability in a business context. We take a closer look at each of these.

Life Cycle Assessment

What is a life cycle assessment (LCA)? It can be a lot of different things, depending on who uses the term, but at its core, it is an attempt to evaluate the environmental aspects of a product or service from the beginning of the product's useful life to its end. Thus, LCA is often called a "cradle to grave" analysis. No matter what the product or service, every company leaves an environmental footprint in its production and distribution, and most companies have completed LCAs for their major operations. One observation these LCAs have led to is, the more pollution the company creates, the larger is its environmental footprint.

The LCA concept has a simple premise: If we know all the environmental impacts of a product or service, we can make better decisions with respect to the environment. Let's use the simple yellow pencil with an eraser as an example. Begin by imagining its extremely simple supply chain. From a pencil manufacturer's perspective, there are only a limited number of component parts and materials— wood, graphite lead, glue, paint, metal ferrule, vinyl eraser, and other components.

The raw materials come into the factory from one side, and finished pencils go out on the other side. As they leave the factory, the finished pencils are packaged, loaded on transportation vehicles such as trucks, and shipped to distributors and customers around the world.

Exhibit 2.1. The Pencil.

In the past, asking the pencil manufacturer to trace its environmental footprint was a request that elicited a straightforward response. The executive would cite environmental impacts that arise from factory operations—exhaust from the equipment on the factory floor, waste water emissions, volatile organic emissions from the paint shop, and scrap wood, metal, and graphite.

All these factors are inputs to the company's LCA, and each factor or process is examined to identify cost-effective alternatives that may be more ecologically efficient. For example, installing solar panels could reduce the amount of greenhouse gases the pencil's manufacture emitted to the atmosphere. The factory's waste water could be treated before its discharge into the nearby stream. And ventilators could be deployed to reduce exposure to volatile organic compounds. By implementing these practices, the pencil factory will become more eco-efficient, that is, more sustainable and more economical, and thereby reduce its environmental footprint.

There is a more comprehensive view of the environmental footprint of the pencil that extends the analysis beyond the strict boundaries of the factory floor. This extended analysis includes the manufacturing process for the pencil, as described above, and added to that are all of the upstream processes conducted by suppliers of the pencil's raw materials— the wood, graphite, paint, glue, eraser, ferrule, and other components. This broader view of LCA also extends the analysis downstream, to the pencil's distribution, its use by customers, and, finally, its ultimate disposal. In this broader view, what happens outside the boundaries of the factory is just as important from an environmental perspective as what happens within the factory's gate.

To gain a full understanding of the pencil's total environmental footprint, we must ask questions about the operations of all of its suppliers going back to the cradle (i.e., raw materials) and extending to the grave (i.e., ultimate disposal, reuse, or recycle). For example, is the supplier of cedar wood harvesting the cedar in a sustainable manner? Have other suppliers adopted better practices? Are the stain, wax, and paint suppliers providing material that is safe for use, considering that consumers may put pencils into their mouths? When the stain, wax, and paint are applied to the pencil, do they produce harmful air emissions which might harm the plant's workers? What about the vinyl used to make the eraser? Does it contain phthalate plasticizers, which have been linked to health concerns, including endocrine disorders, particularly in children? We must also ask questions about the transportation and distribution networks, and the energy and carbon dioxide emissions along the entire supply chain. Finally, what happens to the pencil when it is no longer used? Is it discarded into a landfill? And what is the environmental fate of its parts?

The environmental performance and potential impacts of a product can be measured on many different dimensions, and the choice depends a great deal on the product or service under study. Here is a list of potential effects that can be measured in an LCA:

- Global warming potential (carbon dioxide equivalent emissions)
- Stratospheric ozone depletion
- Water use
- Toxic releases to the air, water, and land
- Resource depletion (energy, minerals, fish stocks, forests)
- Eutrophication (oxygen deficiency) and nutrification (excess nutrients) of water bodies, either of which affects aquatic life

There is no one ideal way to measure environmental impacts in an LCA. Some studies look at impacts on only a single dimension, such as greenhouse gas emissions, whereas others are more comprehensive. Furthermore, the measurement's units differ by the type of impact. Greenhouse gas emissions are typically stated in metric tons (or kilograms) of CO_2 equivalents,[1] whereas carcinogens can be measured in units that consider the impact on life expectancy or quality of life. Two such measures are disability-adjusted life years (DALY)[2] and quality-adjusted life years (QALY).[3] Most LCAs track impacts in physical units; others dollarize these physical units and measure impacts on a monetary scale.

Returning to our yellow pencil example, the LCA reflects the pencil's complete life cycle—from raw materials to manufacture and use, and finally to disposal. In practice, establishing the precise scope and boundaries of an LCA is often difficult, especially when the LCA includes indirect impacts such as emissions of the power plant that generated electricity for the factory, energy use when the consumer uses the product, and the different ways in which products are discarded (recycled, incinerated, or used as landfill).

Some companies prefer a more limited scope for a life cycle analysis. For example, a "cradle to gate" analysis examines the environmental impacts of a product from resource extraction through the manufacturing process. Other companies are interested only in a "gate to gate" analysis, which focuses entirely on the manufacturing process. The broader the scope and the more factors that are considered, the more complete an LCA will be, but the more time and money it will require.

Just as consumers and purchasing agents use Internet services such as Kayak and Orbitz that compare prices for similar products, environmentally conscious consumers can also look online for information regarding the differential impact of various products on the ecosystem. For example, the Environmental Working Group (www.ewg.org) is an NGO whose mission is to provide objective research and education on a range of environmental issues to the public. Their published research includes guides on cosmetics, sunscreens, consumer products, cleaners, and pesticides in food. Another source of consumer information is Good Guide (www.goodguide.com). Good Guide created an application that allows smart phone users to scan a product's bar code and access information on the health, environmental, and social impacts of the product and the company. Listed below are some common product groups. Which option you choose can lead to significantly different environmental impacts.

- Coffee cups. Are ceramic coffee mugs better for the environment than disposable paper or Styrofoam™ cups? The analysis should consider not only the manufacturing cost of each product but also convenience, disposal, water and energy usage, and how much longer the ceramic mug lasts compared to the paper or plastic cup. Hint: The answer probably depends on how long the product will be in service before it is discarded.

Exhibit 2.2. Coffee Mug/Cup.

- Light bulbs. Are compact fluorescent bulbs more sustainable than incandescent or LED bulbs? The analysis should consider the material composition and life expectancy of the bulb and the amount of energy the bulb requires when used. Hint: The answer depends on energy saving over time. CFL bulbs last on average 10 times longer and LED bulbs 25 times longer than traditional incandescent bulbs. However, be aware that the incandescent bulb is being phased out in the United States.
- Carpets. Is a woolen carpet better for the environment than a nylon carpet, a synthetic material derived from oil and natural gas? The LCA should consider the differences in raw material costs, the durability of the materials, and the difference in CO_2 emissions from raising sheep (grazing, burping, manure) compared with the nylon manufacturing process. Hint: Surprisingly, consumers who choose nylon carpets make a decision that is better for the environment. A nylon carpet will emit fewer CO_2 emissions over the life of the product compared to a woolen carpet. Sheep emit a great deal of methane, a potent greenhouse gas.

Exhibit 2.3. CFL Bulb, Incandescent Bulb.

Exhibit 2.4. Nylon Carpet, Sheep Wool Carpet.

- Grocery bags. Are paper grocery sacks more eco-friendly than plastic carry-out bags? The LCA should consider the different manufacturing costs, end of life options (recycle, incineration, landfill), and the weight of the bag (shipping the heavier item to customers will affect the CO_2 emissions in the LCA). Hint: The best answer may be neither one.

- Diapers. Do disposable diapers have a larger environmental footprint than cloth diapers? Hint: Neither product is impact free. Recent studies indicate that these products have very similar impacts on the environment, all things considered.[4]

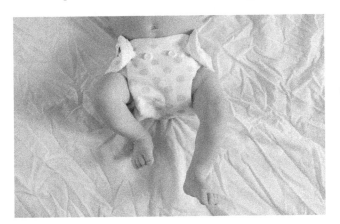

Exhibit 2.5. Baby in Diapers.

Life cycle assessment is an important process for understanding the broad and cumulative impact of products that we purchase. The LCA evaluates all stages of a product's life, and their interdependencies are recognized. No one stage is more or less important than another stage.

An LCA can provide many benefits. A good LCA can highlight the environmental pressure points and help decision makers select the product or process that results in the least harm to the environment and reduces risks to employees and consumers. In addition, manufacturers can use information from the LCA in conjunction with other factors such as cost and performance data to identify cost reduction opportunities while improving the social value the company creates. For example, suppose Wal-Mart is choosing between two rival products: Option 1 is a line of traditional cotton textile products whereas Option 2 uses only organic cotton. By performing an LCA of the cotton textile supply chain, Wal-Mart learns that conventional cotton crops consume more than 25% of all chemical insecticides and more than 10% of chemical pesticides in agriculture.[5] Furthermore, many of these chemicals are suspected carcinogens and, after application on the cotton crop, these chemicals are dispersed into the soil, water, and air. Wal-Mart's use of LCA has helped managers choose the organic cotton, which has "saved time and money, and reduced the environmental impacts associated with this business segment."[6]

Besides choosing less harmful materials in a company's production process, another benefit of a good LCA is that it helps to identify ways to improve resource productivity—for example, energy usage, water consumption, and the amount of waste generated.

A good LCA has many other applications in business. A company's marketing department can use it to decide whether to advertise based on the environmental improvements and benefits of its products and services, and whether these benefits justify a higher price. The purchasing department can use it to decide whether to choose their suppliers solely based on traditional criteria (cost, performance, on-time delivery) and, if yes, what weight to place on environmental criteria. Government procurement bodies have taken the lead in establishing sustainability and environmental standards as a prerequisite for potential suppliers.[7] Corporate procurement systems have made significant progress as well, especially when such policies help them avoid negative public relations. The research and development department (or product design group) can use the LCA to decide whether to modify a product's design to be more environmentally friendly by eliminating potentially harmful materials, and whether to ask component suppliers to do likewise. Within the executive suite, the LCA can be used to benchmark the company's environmental performance over time and compare this performance with others in the industry. Thus, a good LCA will contribute to all aspects of the triple bottom line and not just to improving the environmental footprint.

Some well-publicized examples of LCAs among major corporations include:

- Dow Chemical's program Waste Reduction Always Pays (WRAP), which was designed to stimulate a cultural shift in the thinking of Dow's employees concerning the value of reducing waste releases and emissions.
- 3M's program Pollution Prevention Pays (3P), which is based on the concept that pollution prevention is more environmentally effective, technically sound, and economical than conventional pollution control strategies.

- Frito-Lay's "near net zero" factory in Arizona. Frito-Lay took a production facility "off the grid," running primarily on renewable energy sources and recycled water, while producing nearly zero landfill waste.
- Subaru's zero landfill plant in Indiana, which became the first automotive assembly facility in North America to recycle or reuse all waste and send minimal amounts to the landfill.

In many ways, the eco-efficiency gains highlighted in an LCA represents "low-hanging fruit" for a company. The LCA helps companies improve their environmental performance and typically reduce their costs, at the same time. Retro-fitting plants, installing energy saving devices, and installing centralized controls for heating, lighting, and cooling systems can lead to high returns on investment and short pay-back periods. Some paybacks are within months.

As a result of the input from LCAs, companies have made considerable progress in increasing their eco-efficiency and reducing their carbon and water footprints. Despite this progress, though, modern industrial production is far from perfect. Our consumer-based society faces too many resource constraints and places too many burdens on our environment. The growth of the manufacturing sector in China to serve the export markets in the developed world provides a case in point. The World Bank's detailed study of clean water and clear air resource constraints and the tension between economic growth and the burdens placed on the environment in China concluded:

> In recent decades, China has achieved rapid economic growth, industrialization, and urbanization. . . . Although technological change, urbanization, and China's high savings rate suggest that continued rapid growth is feasible, the resources that such growth demands and the environmental pressures it brings have raised grave concerns about the long-term sustainability and hidden costs of growth. Many of these concerns are associated with the impacts of air and water pollution.[8]

Cradle to Cradle Design

In the face of continuing concerns about long-term environmental sustainability such as the World Bank's with regard to China's growth, architect William McDonough and others have argued that we need to look at environmental issues in a totally new way. Rather than using a "cradle-to-grave" model, McDonough proposes that companies should redesign their products and services to completely close the loop. He calls this cradle-to-cradle design, often designated as C2C. In his 2002 book with Michael Braungart, *Cradle to Cradle: Remaking the Way We Make Things,* he provides guidelines for how companies can achieve this closed loop goal. The book was influential and helped spur a transformation in manufacturing design to encourage the use of safer products that are eventually broken down to become the source materials for new products. Braungart and McDonough envisioned a world in which the reuse of the materials would be better than the previous use. They call these products "upcycled," unlike the common practice of "downcycling" when the next use of the material is downgraded as when a food grade plastics bottle is recycled to become part of fleece outerwear. Recognizing that the sort of revolutionary change they propose will be implemented incrementally in our daily lives, the authors expanded upon their original work in their 2013 book, *The Upcycle: Beyond Sustainability—Designing for Abundance.* This book provides practical illustrations of their efforts to translate theory into practice.

The C2C concept is modeled on nature or biomimetics. Consider the ecosystem of a forest. Trees turn sunlight into food, absorb carbon dioxide, and create oxygen. The tree's root system filters water and its blossoms provide seeds for future generations of trees and food for other living organisms. Its fallen leaves drop to the ground each year and provide nutrition for microorganisms in the soil, which turn the leaves into rich compost to help sustain the trees. The system generates no toxic waste or other harmful materials. One organism's waste cycles through the ecosystem to provide another organism's nutrition. And the process can be repeated over and over again.

In the C2C model, companies are urged to imagine a world of products and services that are re-designed to mimic these natural systems. Here's how it works. In the model's ideal world, products are composed of two primary materials—technical nutrients and biological nutrients. Technical nutrients are inorganic or synthetic materials—such as plastics and metals—that can be used and re-used many times over without any loss in quality. They are limited to nontoxic, nonharmful materials that have no adverse effect on the environment. Biological nutrients are

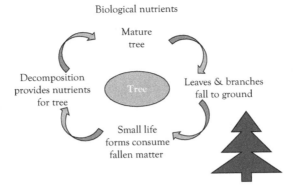

Exhibit 2.6. Biological nutrients.

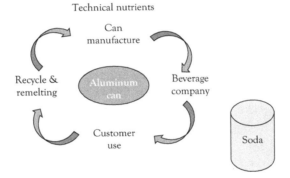

Exhibit 2.7. Technical nutrients.

organic materials that can decompose into the natural environment, like the leaves in the forest. The natural decomposition provides food for bacteria and small life forms without affecting the natural environment. So, focusing on the end of a product's life, which is being disposed of in a landfill, designers have created the product so that it can be broken down into biological nutrients that safely decompose and technical components that can be re-used in other parts of our industrial system. This is shown in Exhibits 2.6 and 2.7. In the C2C model, Waste = Food.[9]

There have been some notable examples of C2C product design over the past decade.

- Nylon 6 is an ideal material for use as a technical nutrient. It is a synthetic material made from caprolactam, which itself is a derivative of oil and natural gas. Traditionally, carpet fiber made from Nylon 6 ends up in a landfill at the end of its useful life. Now, companies like Honeywell, BASF, Collins & Aikman, Desso, Milliken, and Interface have developed programs to take back their carpet from commercial customers for re-use in a closed-loop cycle. Some of these company programs are more sophisticated than others, but at its core, this approach depolymerizes Nylon 6 to caprolactam, which is used again and again. Instead of being discarded in landfills or downcycled to lesser-valued products, recycled Nylon 6 can be converted into products of equal or greater value.

- Nike, the major sportswear and sports equipment supplier, has adopted a number of sustainability initiatives. In the product design area, it has created a line of more sustainable shoes, called Nike Considered. These shoes utilize raw materials that are primarily found within a two-hundred mile radius of the manufacturing plant. The purpose of the near-by sourcing is to reduce the energy and greenhouse gas emissions used in transportation. Nike Considered also reduces solvent use by over 80% compared with other Nike products, uses leather that is dyed with vegetable based colors, uses shoelaces and woven sections made with polyester and hemp for easier recycling, and greatly reduces or eliminates toxic substances and manufacturing waste.

- The Think® chair by Steelcase was developed with C2C principles in mind. It weighs only 32 pounds, is made from up to 44% recycled materials, and contains no hazardous materials (such as PVC, chrome, mercury, or lead). Suppliers send materials to the Think® chair manufacturing plant in reusable totes to reduce packaging waste. At the end of its useful life, the chair is disassembled in about 5 minutes, using common hand tools. Parts weighing more than 50 grams (about 2 ounces) are clearly labeled for recycling.

- Trigema, Germany's largest T-shirt and tennis clothing manufacturer, has been in business for more than 90 years. The company now offers a line of Cradle to Cradle cotton apparel completely free of toxic dyes. At the end of their useful life, the clothing items can be recycled into new garments or processed to provide compost to enhance the soil.

Despite these positive developments, many experts have questioned the practicality of the C2C model and the difficulties in its implementation. Some of the difficulties include the information requirements to fully understand the chemical and material properties of products throughout the supply chain, the cost of C2C certification, and the fact that the C2C model ignores the use phase of a product (e.g. a lightweight car will be more fuel efficient than a much heavier vehicle). Nevertheless, the C2C model provides an excellent starting point for many new product innovations.

Resources on Sustainability Systems for Students

Here is a collection of online resources on sustainability that we have found useful. Those that require subscription for access are often available in university databases, so check with your librarian.

- "Life Cycle Assessment: Principles and Practice," a report for the U.S. Environmental Protection Agency, 2006 (http://www.epa.gov/nrmrl/std/lca/lca.html)
- International Standards Organization, ISO 14040 "Environmental management—Life cycle assessment—Principles and Framework," 2006 (available for purchase from iso.org)
- *The International Journal of Life Cycle Assessment* (http://www.springer.com/environment/journal/11367)
- *Journal of Industrial Ecology* (http://onlinelibrary.wiley.com/ journal/10.1111/%28ISSN%291530-9290)
- Sustainable Minds (www.sustainableminds.com)
- EcoInvent database (www.ecoinvent.org/database)

Assessment and Measurement Tools

Now that we've reviewed two of the conceptual systems available to use in thinking about sustainability in the business context, we are ready to take a look at how we measure sustainability and assess the results of our sustainability efforts. Every student who has passed through Management 101 knows that management requires measurement and that its key challenge is to find a meaningful unit of measure across different sectors that can serve as a common yardstick. Three widely recognized indicators related to sustainability measure quite different things:

- Operational indicators track stresses a business creates on the environment, such as by burning coal or emitting gasses.
- Management indicators are concerned with what actions companies take to reduce their impacts on the environment, such as recycling and sustainable sourcing.
- Environment condition indicators measure aspects of the environment's quality, such as air pollution or glacier melt.[10]

These indicators are related. Management indicators, such as tracking the time spent on environmental training, are internal to the firm and may influence operational indicators, such as the use of electricity or fossil fuel. The operational indicators function to link the firm's actions with the outside world. For example, a reduction in the firm's use of fossil fuel would influence environment condition indicators, such as average global temperatures, greenhouse gas emissions, and average sea level rise.[11]

From a global perspective, we see several trends in environmental reporting. One is that in some countries, governments have begun to impose legal obligations on firms. For example, the European Union (EU) requires that companies with industrial emissions apply the best available techniques to their processes, cause no significant pollution, maximize energy efficiency, reduce waste, and conduct any remediation necessary. Another trend is the call for increased transparency on environmental issues. For example, in November 2012, China saw public protests against pollution, to which the government responded with increased transparency on sustainability measures. Trends such as these push the public's expectations forward, and once firms begin reporting, stakeholders ask for more—more information, more verification, and more comparable information.[12]

Corporate Sustainability Reporting Systems

The purpose of sustainability reporting is to provide a mechanism so that organizations can measure their performance on four sustainability dimensions (economic, environmental, social, and governance performance) and communicate about their performance to stakeholders and others. The basic idea that drives sustainability reporting is the desire to make it as reliable and comparable across companies as financial reporting. The two most commonly used reporting platforms in corporate sustainability reporting are the UN Global Compact and the Global Reporting Initiative (GRI), and, fortunately, they have aligned as strategic partners. In addition to the GRI and the Global Compact, another commonly used corporate reporting system is the Carbon Disclosure Project (CDP), a reporting system developed by a British organization whose focus is on corporate reporting of greenhouse gas emissions and, more recently, water data. CDP's basic model is based on collaborative membership, and they have been successful in building major corporate membership. There are also some efforts to measure carbon and water use and discharge, a process called footprinting. Here, once we look at the theory on which measurement of corporate actions on the environment rests, we describe each of these organizations and efforts, and their contributions to the measurement of corporate sustainability.

The theoretical basis for measuring the impact of activities on the environment is based on the work of Herman E. Daley, former chief economist at the World Bank. His work draws on the thinking of economist Nicholas Georgescu-Roegen, author of *The Entropy Law and the Economic Process*, and establishes a set of rules to support ecological sustainability. Now commonly known as the Daley Rules, they are:

1. Renewable resources such as fish, soil, and groundwater must be used no faster than the rate at which they regenerate.
2. Nonrenewable resources such as minerals and fossil fuels must be used no faster than the rate at which renewable substitutes for them can be put in place.
3. Pollution and wastes must be emitted no faster than natural systems can absorb them, recycle them, or render them harmless.[13]

The two organizations whose environmental reports offer a model and so merit our initial attention are the United Nations Global Compact and the Global Reporting Initiative. The United Nations Global Compact (UNglobalcompact.org) is of interest because it maintains the largest database of corporate environmental sustainability reports and it draws on the social capital of the UN member states to encourage companies to report. The Global Reporting Initiative (GRI) is the most commonly used framework and is a collaboration of many different stakeholders at many different levels. The Global Compact actually uses the GRI framework for its reporting.

The Global Compact

The United Nations Global Compact is an agreement among businesses begun in 2000 at the urging of then UN Secretary-General Kofi Annan. The Compact addresses four basic areas—human rights, labor, environment, and anti-corruption—with the goal of providing benefits to businesses, societies, and economies everywhere. In joining the Compact, businesses agree to develop strategies that support the Compact's ten principles, three of which concern the environment: A precautionary approach to environmental challenges, initiatives to promote greater environmental responsibility, and encouragement of the development and diffusion of environmentally friendly technologies.[14]

The Global Compact now has over 8,700 corporate members from 135 countries, each of whom pledges to file an annual report, which makes it the world's largest corporate responsibility initiative. Along with its corporate members, the Global Compact has academic, civil society, labor, public sector, and city members. It provides a framework for "the development, implementation, and disclosure of sustainability policies and practices, offering participants a wide spectrum of workstreams, management tools, and resources—all designed to help advance sustainable business models and markets."[15] The Global Compact is voluntary and self-defines as "a complement rather than a substitute for regulatory regimes."

The Global Compact is still in its formative stages. Its executive director, Goerg Kell, reports that 40% of the 500 largest global companies

THE TEN PRINCIPLES OF THE GLOBAL COMPACT

RESPECT
and support
internationally
proclaimed
human rights
in its area of
influence

MAKE SURE
the company
is not complicit
with human
rights abuses

UPHOLD
the freedom
of association
and recognize
the right to
collective
bargaining

ELIMINATE
all forms
of forced or
compulsory
labor

EFFECTIVELY
eradicate all
forms of child
labor from its
productive chain

ELIMINATE
discrimination
in respect of
employment
and occupation

SUPORT
a precautionary,
responsible, and
proactive approach
to environmental
challenges

UNDERTAKE
initiatives and
practices to
promote and
disseminate
environmental
responsibility

ENCOURAGE
the development
and dissemination
of environmentally
friendly
technologies

WORK AGAINST
corruption in
all its forms,
including
extortion
and bribery

Exhibit 2.8. UN Global Compact: Ten Principles.

Source: United Nations Global Compact (n.d.).

are members, a figure that constitutes 10% of all multinationals. To put these figures in context, of the world's 10 largest companies identified by market capitalization at the end of the second quarter of 2012, six were members of the Global Compact. Of 4,000 companies that submitted Global Compact annual reports during the last year, Kell observed that 5% were judged to be at advanced levels of reporting, suggesting that leaders in environmental reporting are still a scarce commodity.[16]

The Global Compact requires its corporate members to file an annual report on their transparency and accountability known as the Communication on Progress (COP). The content of the COP needs to suggest a serious and committed engagement with sustainability. According to a report in *The Guardian*,[17] Executive Director Kell has delisted 3,100 Global Compact businesses members for their commitment to greenwashing in lieu of sustainability. Kell stresses that the Global Compact's basic intent is to represent a corporation's serious commitment to sustainability *as a way to survive*, not as a public relations activity. He described the delisted companies as "free riders who joined but had no intention to stay engaged."

In the spring of 2010, the Global Compact aligned with the Global Reporting Initiative, a solid step forward for both organizations. The Global Compact has adapted the Global Reporting Initiative's framework, initially as an option, for the COP. This collaboration increases the Compact's value as a standard measure. We look next at this framework that has contributed to the Global Compact's relevance.

The Global Reporting Initiative (GRI)

The GRI is a networked organization of a broad array of stakeholders, including its core supporters, who together have developed this most widely used sustainability reporting framework. The origin of the GRI is found in the efforts of two Boston nonprofits, the Coalition for Environmentally Responsible Economies (CERES) and the Tellus Institute, who worked together beginning in 1997 to develop a reporting framework that would be widely accepted. Initial stakeholders included corporate, public, academic, and governmental representatives. When this framework received a positive reception in 2000, CERES built a partnership for the GRI with the United Nations Environmental Program. CERES then spun off the GRI so that it would exist as a separate institution, and today it is headquartered in Amsterdam. Thousands of companies use the GRI framework to report their environmental impacts.

GRI's Sustainability Reporting Guidelines contain a clear statement of principles and a set of disclosure items, in order to define the contents of the report. The current version, the GRI Guidelines 3.1, was introduced in 2011, and there is an early draft of Guidelines 4, which will be circulated for comment and then edited, based on the response of various stakeholders. There are two main parts of Guidelines 3.1: A detailed section on how to report and a similarly detailed section on what should be reported, including management disclosures and performance indicators. The performance indicators cover three broad categories, economic, environment, and social. The social category includes labor, human rights, social, and product responsibility. Every Performance Indicator (PI) has Indicator Protocols (IP) that function as its recipe: Definitions, directions on how to compile the data, their scope and relevance, and references. The GRI has a total of thirty Environmental Performance Indicators divided into eight aspects—Materials; Energy; Water; Biodiversity; Emissions, Effluents, and Waste; Products and Services; Compliance; Transport—and an overall summary.

This sounds quite complicated, and in aggregate, it is. But at the level of an individual indicator, the GRI's precision makes possible comparisons among the various reporting firms. For example, the GRI Performance Indicator EN10 Water measures the total volume of water recycled and reused. It describes the relevance of the measure, gives a description of how to compile the measure, what water to include (both treated and untreated water, and water based on the demands of production, so recycled water is included in the calculation as many times as it is used), what measures to use (cubic meters per year), what constitutes recycling, and documentation (water bills, water meters, a water retailer). EN13 Biodiversity measures the habitats protected or restored. Again, the performance indicator describes the relevance of the measure, how to compile it, appropriate definitions, documentation, and references. In addition to these performance indicators, there are supplements for different industry sectors and nations so that the framework will meet the varying needs of

Exhibit 2.9. Membership in United Nations Global Compact

Ten largest corporations	Membership global compact	GRI participation
Apple	No	Yes
China Mobile Communications	Yes	Yes
Exxon	No	Yes
General Electric	Yes	Yes
IBM	No	Yes
Industrial and Commercial Bank of China	Yes	Yes
Microsoft	Yes	Yes
PetroChina	Yes	Yes
Royal Dutch Shell	Yes	Yes
Walmart	No	Yes

its broad range of users. You can find examples of the GRI framework at globalreporting.org.[18]

There are three more reporting initiatives that merit our focus, the Carbon Disclosure Project or CDC, carbon footprinting and water footprinting. We now look at these.

Carbon Disclosure Project or CDP

The Carbon Disclosure Project,[19] which recently changed its name to CDP to reflect the growth of its concerns beyond carbon, is a U.K.-based nonprofit that focuses on the reduction of greenhouse gas emissions and sustainable water use. Just as GRI has developed a major sustainability reporting standard, CDP appears to be on its way to providing the major standards for carbon emissions reporting. The CDP's basic approach is to partner with global organizations and, more recently, cities, a marked contrast from the nation-based efforts of the UN's Kyoto Protocol. CDP has been successful in building partnerships with major corporations and providing them with emissions reporting standards. Over 85% of the global 500 corporations report their emissions to the CDP and use CDP to set targets and to improve their environmental impacts. CDP's supply chain program has supported companies such as IBM and HP in

Exhibit 2.10. Climate Disclosure Leadership Index Scores, 2012: Consumer Discretionary and Consumer Staples Categories

Sector	Company	Disclosure score	Years in CDLI	Performance band
Consumer Discretionary	BMW	99	2	A
	Daimler	99	1	A-
	Philips Electronics	98	2	A-
	TJX Companies	97	1	B
	Honda Motor	96	1	B
	Panasonic	96	3	A
	Home Depot	95	1	B
	News Corp.	95	3	B
Consumer Staples	Nestlé	100	3	A
	Diageo	98	1	A
	Danone	97	1	B
	Coca Cola	96	1	B
	L'Oreal	94	1	B
	PepsiCo	94	2	B

Source: Data and report structure from Carbon Disclosure Project at https://www.cdproject.net

their efforts to require their suppliers to disclose emissions to continue as suppliers and has led to CDP fast becoming the price of doing business with many global corporations.[20] They recently have expanded their focus beyond carbon concerns to include water, forests, and climate change.

CDP's five major programs all encourage reduction in greenhouse gas emissions, each with a separate focus:, investors, public procurement, water, supply chain, and cities. CDP also provides an annual Carbon Disclosure Leadership Index to recognize and reward companies with quality disclosure processes and performance. Data from the 2012 Index can be found in Exhibit 2.10. Standards and questionnaires for these disclosure reports by sector (auto, electric utilities, oil and gas, ICT) are available on the CDP's web site. The disclosure score is based on the company's disclosure and the performance band rating is based on performance. So a high disclosure score indicates that the company's response is comprehensive and shows "clear consideration of business-specific risks and potential opportunities related to climate change and good internal data management practices for understanding GHG (green house gas) emissions."[21] Note that this score does not reflect what a company is doing to mitigate climate change. The performance band measures the actions the company has taken to mitigate climate change along with the adaptation they have made and their transparency.

Linkage between CDP and GRI is underway so that reporting guidelines will be the same for both frameworks, as they are with GRI and the Global Compact.

Carbon Footprinting

Another measurement process that businesses are beginning to use to measure their sustainability efforts is carbon footprinting. On a conceptual level, it is fairly straightforward to define as the total set of greenhouse gas emissions caused by a product. On a practical level, however, calculating the total carbon footprint is quite difficult, because of the large amount of data required and because carbon dioxide can be produced by natural occurrences. Calculation of the carbon footprint is even more difficult if the boundary conditions constitute not a product but an entire factory, or a diversified company, or a city. Following the guidance of experts in the field like Wright, Kemp, and Williams,[22] we suggest here a more workable definition: The carbon footprint of a product is a measure of the total amount of carbon dioxide emissions that includes all relevant sources, sinks, and storage within the spatial and temporal boundaries of the product (or system). It is calculated as the carbon dioxide equivalent (denoted CO_2e) using the relevant 100-year global warming potential.

In most contexts, the goal is to measure the carbon footprint of a product throughout the life cycle of that product, from cradle to grave. Greenhouse gases can be emitted at every stage of the life cycle, which includes during raw material extraction, production, transportation, land clearance, and use. In calculating the carbon footprint, both direct and indirect sources of carbon emissions need to be considered. For example, when we drive an automobile, we emit carbon dioxide directly into the atmosphere. We also indirectly emit carbon dioxide because many of the automobile's components—steel, glass, aluminum, and plastics—use fossil fuels and electrical energy in their manufacture, processing, and

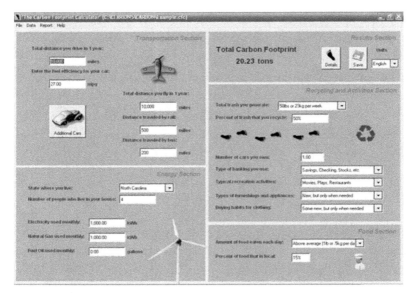

Exhibit 2.11. Calculating your personal carbon footprint.
Source: http://fileforum.betanews.com/detail/Carbon-Footprint-Calculator/1206132265/1

transportation. These emissions are considered indirect and are included in the carbon footprint analysis. For the average household, in fact, most of the carbon footprint emissions come from these indirect sources. To become more aware of your personal contribution to greenhouse gas emissions, you may wish to use a calculator like the one shown in Exhibit 2.11.

Consider the following example of how carbon footprinting can support corporate sustainability efforts. Frito-Lay, a division of PepsiCo, Inc., the leading supplier of snack foods in the United States, achieved some important milestones in 2011 in taking its Casa Grande, Arizona manufacturing plant "off the grid" through the installation of the latest energy saving and water saving technologies. The plant makes Lay's Potato Chips, Doritos tortilla chips, Fritos corn chips, and Cheetos cheese flavored snacks. The plant uses energy in two principal forms: Natural gas (direct CO_2e emissions) from their local pipeline supplier and electricity from the grid (indirect CO_2e emissions). The energy is used to power production equipment, heat ovens, and heat cooking oil. The company also uses water from the local water utility. After the energy upgrades were

Exhibit 2.12. Global Warming Potential for Various Gases

Gas	Lifetime	GWP—100 year
Methane	12	25
Nitrous oxide	114	298
HFC-23	270	14,800
HFC-134a	14	1,430
Sulfur hexafluoride	3,200	22,800

Source: Intergovernmental Panel on Climate Change, Fourth Assessment Report, Working Group 1, Chapter 2, p. 212.

installed, the company achieved an 80% reduction in natural gas consumption, a 50% reduction in greenhouse gas emissions, between 50% and 75% of its water is recycled, and less than 1% of its overall waste goes to the landfill. Frito-Lay calls this plan the *Net Zero Plan*.

In addition to carbon dioxide, we need to consider a number of other gases that contribute to global warming and are used to calculate the carbon footprint of a product. For simplicity, all these other gases are compared with the global warming potential of carbon dioxide based on a 100-year atmospheric lifespan (by way of explanation, many of these gases do not degrade significantly for that long a time frame). Methane, for example, has a global warming potential (GWP) of 25 compared to carbon dioxide's (GWP) of 1. This means that emissions of 1 million tons of methane are equivalent to emissions of 25 million tons of carbon dioxide. Exhibit 2.12 shows the global warming potential for a number of gases.

Water Footprinting

Over the past several years, we have developed a better understanding of our carbon footprint, which has led to the recognition that carbon, climate change, and water are inextricably linked. Yet the impacts of changing patterns of water availability are neither recognized nor well appreciated by most businesses and consumers. Demand for water is increasing because of a rapidly growing world population and changing patterns of consumption, whereas water supply is threatened by climate change and human activities that lead to polluted water. The impacts of climate change include changes in patterns of precipitation (too much rainfall in some regions, too little rainfall in others), reduced formation of glaciers, and increased concentration of salts in aquifers. In many parts of the world, we have consistently under priced water, because of which it has been wasted and over-used. Several organizations, including the CDP (formerly the Carbon Disclosure Project), are responding to investor and business concerns about this issue by creating a reporting system for companies to measure and report their water footprint.

Measuring and reporting water availability and usage is a more complex process than is that for carbon dioxide. First, water is a local as well as a global issue. It does not matter whether carbon dioxide emissions occurred in California or China, they both contribute equally to environmental impacts. It matters a great deal, on the other hand, whether water is extracted from Phoenix (a water-short region) or Philadelphia (a water-rich region). Second, the source and use of water also matter a great deal. Ample rainfall will replenish water supplies; removal of water from aquifers in drought-stricken regions may require decades, or even millennia, to replenish.

Because of its intricacies, the methodology for water footprinting is not as well developed as is the methodology for carbon footprinting. First of all, the global nature of business and the intricate web of suppliers that use water across multiple geographies make the challenge of tracking the water footprint complex. Furthermore, obtaining reliable data on water usage and water quality represents another challenge. CDP has recently introduced a water disclosure process aimed at improving water use measurement, setting benchmarks, and providing data to stakeholders. CDP is also presently developing a methodology for scoring.

Against this background, the concept of measuring water use along supply chains has gathered momentum over the past decade. The water footprint, defined as the total volume of water used to produce a product over the full supply chain, looks at *direct* water use as well as *indirect* use. It is a multidimensional indicator that shows water use by source and polluted volume of water created by the production process. It often segments water use by type: Blue water is fresh water from surface and underground sources; green water is water from rainfall; and grey water is polluted water from the production process.

In our initial review of the Global Reporting Initiative, we looked at the performance indicators of recycled and reused water to illustrate the efforts GRI is making to standardize measurement. Overall, GRI uses five standards for companies to report their water-related activities. They are:

- Total water withdrawal by source
- Water sources significantly affected by withdrawal of water
- Percentage and total volume of water recycled and reused
- Total water discharge by quality and destination
- Identity, size, protected status, and biodiversity value of water bodies significantly affected by the reporting organization's discharges of water and runoff

Let's look at the water footprint of a 16.9 fluid ounce bottle of soda. Its water footprint depends on its ingredients, and these vary by manufacturer. The production of a soft drink typically includes the following process steps: Produce and form the plastic bottle, clean the bottle, prepare the syrup, mix, fill the bottle, label, and pack. A nondiet soft drink contains sugar, and sugar is derived from three general sources, beet sugar, cane sugar, and high fructose corn syrup (HFCS). Each type of sugar has a significantly different impact on the total water footprint of the soft drink. For example, the total water footprint of the 16.9 oz. soft drink is 82 gallons (310 liters) when the sugar originates from cane sugar, 45 gallons (170 liters) when the sugar comes from beet sugar and 47 gallons (180 liters) when the sugar's source is HFCS. Most of the total water footprint of the soft drink comes from its supply chain, mainly from its ingredients (95%). A smaller fraction stems from packaging and labeling materials (4%), particularly from its bottle. The amount of water consumed in producing the final product is 1% of the water consumed in the supply chain. Note that the production stage water consumption is mainly water incorporated into the product itself. The total water footprint, therefore, is estimated between 45 and 82 gallons per 16.9 fluid ounce soda bottle. In other words, for every ounce of soda in the bottle, between 340 and 720 ounces of water are required.[23]

Water footprint assessment can be instrumental in helping us understand how activities and products relate to water scarcity and pollution,

Exhibit 2.13. Glass/Bottle of Soda.

and what steps might be necessary to ensure that such activities and products do not contribute to unsustainable use of water resources. Companies and investors utilize this tool to better appreciate how water availability may impact company operations. Water foot printing also can be used to drive companies to mitigate risks related to water use and to seize water-related opportunities.

In addition to these efforts to measure sustainability, there are other indexes that focus on various specialized areas of sustainability. Here we briefly review the two most widely recognized of them, both developed by the UN: The Human Development Index and the Human Sustainability Index.

Other United Nations Indexes on Sustainability

The Human Development Index (HDI) measures life expectancy, education, and income. Developed by Mahbub ul Haq, economist, Finance Minister of Pakistan, and advisor to the United Nations Development Programme, the HDI provides a human-centered measure of well-being, an alternative or additional view of the gross national product (GNP). Ul

Haq observed that often times, GNP does not measure the things that make the most difference to peoples' lives:

> The basic purpose of development is to enlarge people's choices. In principle, these choices can be infinite and can change over time. People often value achievements that do not show up at all, or not immediately, in income or growth figures: greater access to knowledge, better nutrition and health services, more secure livelihoods, security against crime and physical violence, satisfying leisure hours, political and cultural freedoms and sense of participation in community activities. The objective of development is to create an enabling environment for people to enjoy long, healthy and creative lives.[24]

You can review the components of the HDI and how they are measured, as well as review the index itself at http://hdr.undp.org/en/statistics/hdi/, which has an interactive section so that you can compare specific measures across countries. Below are some sample data extracted from the 2011 HDI report.

Exhibit 2.14. Sample HDI Data, Highest, Lowest, and World, 2011

HDI Rank	HDI Value	Life expect. at birth	Mean yrs. of schooling	Expected years of schooling	GNI/capita (2005 PPP $)
1. Norway	0.943	81.1	12.6	17.3	47,557
2. Australia	0.929	81.9	12.0	18	34,431
3. Netherlands	0.910	80.7	11.6	16.8	36,402
4. United States	0.910	78.5	12.4	16	43,017
5. New Zealand	0.980	80.7	12.5	18	23,737
6. Canada	0.980	81.0	12.1	16	35,166
182. Liberia	0.329	56.8	3.9	11	265
183. Chad	0.328	49.6	1.5	7.2	1,105
184. Mozambique	0.322	50.2	1.2	9.2	898
185. Burundi	0.316	50.4	2.7	10.5	368
186. Niger	0.295	54.7	1.4	4.9	641
187. D. R. Congo	0.286	48.4	3.5	8.2	280
World	0.682	69.8	7.4	11.3	10,082

Source: United Nations, Human Development Index, http://hdr.undp.org/en/statistics/hdi/

The United Nations Development Programme (UNDP) also has developed a template for an index that measures rates of human development and its costs, that is, the costs that future generations will encounter. This Human Sustainability Index will address three key issues: Connecting today's choices with future choices, measuring the use of environmental resources, and linking the use of local and global resources.[25] Of significant note is that the Human Sustainability Index, along with the HDI, offers an alternative to measuring progress based on growth. The Human Sustainability Index effort was announced at the Rio + 20 conference in Brazil in 2012 and is presently underway.

In our focus on the measurement of sustainability efforts, we looked initially at the Global Compact and GRI, and then at the CDP. In addition, we reviewed the developing efforts at carbon footprinting and, more recently, water footprinting. Then we briefly reviewed two UN indexes that measure wellbeing based on alternatives to the GDP, the Human Development Index and the Human Sustainability Index. You would be right to conclude that there are many approaches to measuring our efforts at sustainability. In fact, the organization International Corporate Sustainability Reporting (enviroreporting.com) lists and explains contemporary frameworks that are in use at present. You may want to consult it if you are interested in exploring the many additional frameworks available for sustainability reporting. Having examined the ways companies can measure and report their efforts at sustainability, we now look at the transparency of their reporting on sustainability.

Transparency of Companies on Environmental Processes

Transparency in sustainability involves the company's public disclosure of information in areas related to sustainability. In the financial area, for example, we have come to expect transparency and openness about corporate governance and performance results. This is largely through the Regulation Fair Disclosure (promulgated in 2000), through which the Security and Exchange Commission required publicly traded companies to disclose information to all investors at the same time and the Sarbanes-Oxley Act (passed in 2002), which legislated a new set of requirements for corporate behavior in governance: Audit independence and financial reporting that stipulated violations would incur criminal liability. One basic assumption that underlies all transparency is that it reduces illegal and unethical behavior.[26]

These regulated and legislated calls for financial transparency were soon matched by calls for corporate social and environmental transparency. Transparency related to sustainability, though, has been motivated largely by stakeholders other than the government. Potential investors want to be able to assess liability and positioning for an inevitable future, and potential consumers want to know how the production of what they consume affects our environment.

The Role of Stakeholder Theory

The idea that transparency leads to better behavior suggests that a corporation's responsibility and duty are to its stakeholders, all those who are affected or influenced by the corporation, rather than more exclusively to its owners or shareholders. R. Edward Freeman developed stakeholder theory in his *Strategic Management: A Stakeholder Approach* and the difference in accountability his theory describes, from shareholders to stakeholders may seem a small change, but it actually leads to considerable modification in how we think about the purpose of business. If a wide group of stakeholder interests is at the center of the business, then the major interest of shareholders, which is return on their investment, or profits, become less central. Yet, of course, they are still necessary, but they no longer hold the exclusive centrality they had before transparency led to the increased role of stakeholders. Especially in the United States, this understanding of the purpose of business is slowly earning acceptance. In the EU, that business has larger social responsibilities related to a wide array of stakeholders has been long the case.

Triple Bottom Line: Meaning and Origins

To discuss transparency in sustainability, measure sustainability performance and compare it across companies, a standardized reporting system that reports sustainability results along with financial results is needed. The triple bottom line concept aims to meet this need because it expands the business metaphor of the bottom line (economic profit) to include the social and environmental bottom lines. John Elkington is usually credited with coining the term "triple bottom line" (or 3BL or TBL, and sometimes referred to as people, profits, and planet) in his 1999 investigation of corporate sustainability, *Cannibals with Forks: The Triple Bottom Line of 21st Century Business.* This title is a reference to the Polish poet Stanislaw Lec's question, "Is it progress if a cannibal uses a fork?" Elkington wondered if holding corporations responsible for reporting on the 3BL would actually constitute progress. Andy Savitz, in his *The Triple Bottom Line*, says that the TBL "captures the essence of sustainability by measuring the impact of an organization's activities on the world . . . including both its profitability and shareholder values and its social, human and environmental capital." Below is a summary of the Savitz explanation of 3BL's comprehensiveness.

Savitz shows that sustainable approaches such as those the 3BL describes make financial sense because they help a company focus on emerging values and demands. He sees 3BL as essentially "the art of doing business in an interdependent world."

The issues of what framework to use for each of the 3BL measures and how to measure results may become concerns at times. For the economic bottom line in the United States, the Generally Accepted Accounting Principles (GAAP), the framework used for financial accounting, are widely accepted. GAAP provides a solid basis for the measurement of economic results. As we move toward global harmonization of accounting standards, the International Financial Reporting Standards (IFRS), followed by most other countries, will play an increasing role in this area. The measures for environmental results also tend to be quantified and standardized as well, as we have seen in our review of the measurement

Exhibit 2.15. Savitz on the Triple Bottom Line

Economic	Social	Environmental
Financial results	Community impact	Air quality
Taxes	Labor practices	Water quality
Monetary flows	Human rights	Energy use
Jobs created	Product responsibility	Waste

Source: Savitz (2006), p. xiii.

tools such as the Global Reporting Initiative (GRI). That is not fully the case for the social impacts of corporate activities, though. GRI does provide the most respected framework for the three areas of 3BL reporting. Version G3 includes indicators for economic, environmental, and social performance (such issues as labor practices, human rights, product responsibility), along with indicators for specific industries, but the GRI metrics are not always fully comparable.

Results of Reporting

We have established the need to report social and environmental results along with economic results, and we have reviewed the frameworks used to do so. Now comes the critical, "So what?" question: What are the results of this reporting? Research into reported results shows that as companies adopt 3BL, their transparency efforts add value to their relationships with their stakeholders, including customers, employees, shareholders, directors, and other companies.[27]

In addition, companies appear to be learning that sustainability practices and their reporting to the public can make business sense beyond stakeholder relationships. The exercises themselves make operational sense, and their reporting yields best practices data for other companies, along with reputation reinforcement. The 2011 McKinsey report on sustainability, *The Business of Sustainability*, points out that companies are recognizing the advantages sustainability can bring to their businesses. This survey discloses that cost savings, process improvement, growth, and value can improve as a result of sustainable operations. McKinsey identifies three key drivers that lead to increased value: Growth, ROI and Risk Management: "Waste Management added waste reduction to their product line to achieve Growth. Dow and Walmart increased return on capital by reducing expenses through improved global-supply chains, facility improvements and manufacturing waste reduction efforts. Nestlé launched a program to promote sustainable cocoa as a risk management effort."[28] Exhibit 2.16 shows how growth, ROI, and risk management support positive business results, as shown in the McKinsey report.

Gwendolyn White outlines the benefits of sustainability reporting and categorizes them into internal and external factors in her *Sustainability*

Exhibit 2.16. Ways Sustainability Leads to Capturing Increased Value

Growth	Risk management	Return on capital
Innovation, New Products	Reputation	Sustainable value chain
New Customers and Markets	Regulations	Sustainable operations
Business Portfolio	Operations Risks	Sales and marketing on green appeal

Source: Data from Bonini and Gorner (2011).

Reporting.[29] One of the internal benefits to the organization she cites for sustainability reporting is a unity that connects strategy (what the company says it wants to do) with outcomes (what it does). Reporting also enables the company to identify areas of potential cost savings that can be gained by efficiencies in the use of energy, water, and materials. These increased efficiencies can lead to financial savings. White also points out that organizational rewards are achieved when all members of the firm buy into the framework of accountability that the reporting process establishes. The external benefits she lists include positive impacts on reputation, which can carry with it further financial benefits and increased connection with stakeholders.

Now that we've looked at the results of increased transparency in reporting, we go on to focus on how financial institutions evaluate the sustainability efforts of companies.

Financial Institutions: Evaluation of Company Sustainability Efforts

When companies report their sustainability results in ways that allow for comparisons, the information can be used as investment criteria. Index funds, which are simply groups of stocks that exemplify a specific sector of the market (e.g., the Dow Jones Industrial Average or the S&P 500 Index) have been created using the results of environmental screening. There are several indexes that focus on high-performing sustainable businesses. They are described in detail in White's *Sustainable Reporting*, and include the FTSE KLD 400 Social Index, the Dow Jones Sustainability Indexes, and SAM (formerly known as Sustainable Asset Management).

In general, these indices differ from the socially responsible investing (SRI) group in that they categorize companies based on their financial, social, and environmental results, rather than on their product category. So there is no filtering of weapons, tobacco, and alcohol companies. The DJSI includes British American Tobacco and Heineken. One way to think of this is that the company's results, social, environmental, and economic, replace the SRI's concern with moral values.

The FTSE KLD 400 Social Index, formerly the Domini 400 Social Index, is made up of 400 companies selected for community relations, diversity, employee relations, human rights, product quality and safety, and environment and corporate governance. The FSTE KLD 400 regularly outperforms the Dow Jones Index.

The Dow Jones Sustainability Indexes (DJSI) are a family of indexes composed of companies chosen from among the companies listed on the Dow Jones Total Global Stock Market Index, based on their sustainability reporting and their long term economic, social, and environmental asset management plans. The indices include the Dow Jones World, various geographic-based indexes (Europe, Nordic, and North America), and industry-specific indexes. In 2012, DJSI combined with the S&P indices to offer an even broader range of participating companies.

The final sustainability indexed funds we look at are run by SAM, headquartered in Zurich, Switzerland, a holding company that includes sustainability indices, asset management, and private equity. SAM partnered with Dow Jones to launch the DJSI in 1999 and, since their merger in 2012, works with the S&P Dow Jones Indices to produce the DJSI. In 2001, SAM developed the first global sustainable water fund.

Summary

The primary goal of this chapter is to set the foundation for ways to think about sustainability as a process and then, for ways to measure our efforts at building sustainable businesses. We reviewed life cycle assessment and cradle to cradle design as cognitive systems that help us integrate sustainable thinking into our business activities. Then we examined the tools that have been developed to measure and assess sustainability efforts. These include the Global Reporting Initiative, the Global Compact, the

Carbon Disclosure Project, carbon and water footprinting, other UN sustainability indexes, company efforts to measure their own sustainability such as the triple bottom line, and various indexed funds developed by the finance industry to evaluate company sustainability efforts. Below, we comment on this chapter's material from varying business functional perspectives.

General Management

The message of "Chapter Two: Systems and Tools for Sustainability" for management is that there are ways to think about the introduction of sustainability and the tools for measuring and discussing sustainability efforts are, in some areas, well developed, and developing in others. The general manager should know that there are many other companies—including competitor firms—walking the sustainability trail along with her, so there is ample opportunity for dialogue, training, and learning from others

Operations

Knowledge of the results of sustainability efforts offers operations managers a way to capture increased value through the creation of products that use nonpolluting manufacturing processes while conserving energy, water, and other natural resources, in a word, they become more eco-efficient. Sustainability also offers reduced risks when associated with production and manufacturing-related liabilities. In Chapter 4 we summarize several examples (Clorox, Herman Miller) centered on the benefits, costs, and risks associated with operational issues.

Entrepreneurship

Sustainability approaches invite the development of new products, new customers, and innovative business models. With these creative approaches, the world's problems are turned into business opportunities. These problems include health, water and sanitation, chemicals, and food and agriculture. In Chapter 4 we highlight several examples of entrepreneurial activities with sustainability as a core value—Burt's Bees, Whole Foods, Molten Metal Technology, and Social Entrepreneurs.

Marketing

Marketing managers often face a dilemma. If they tout the sustainability benefits of a company's products too loudly or flagrantly, they will be accused of greenwashing. If they are silent about the demonstrated sustainability benefits, they may be missing an opportunity to attract customers who care a great deal about sustainability and may even be willing to pay more for such benefits. In Chapter 4, we summarize business cases in which both types of marketing issues arise: FIJI Water, Clorox, Herman Miller, and NextEra.

Supply Chain

Supply chain professionals in global enterprises know that improvements in the sustainability of their logistics operations are essential to long-term profitability. Key areas of concern include environmental issues, risk management and resilience, and reducing waste. In Chapter 4, we highlight several examples that focus on supply chain issues and sustainability: McDonald's, Wal-Mart, and Metropolitan Water.

Finance

Finance and accounting professionals typically ask questions about a project's payback or the return on investment, and they are increasingly adopting global standards for environmental risk management. Internal projects to improve profitability in operations and in the supply chain, generally, do require special financial treatment. In addition, business models that create innovative new products and services or target highly-valued customer market segments can enhance profitability and enterprise value. In Chapter 4 we examine several examples that center on the issue of sustainability and finance: Frito-Lay, Patagonia, NextEra, and Wind Energy.

Going Forward to Chapter 3

We now move forward in "Chapter 3: Thinking About Major Sustainable Issues," to examine some of the major arguments around sustainability issues today. We encourage you to get involved with your opinions and the evidence, remembering to be open to new ways of thinking about things!

CHAPTER 3

Thinking About Major Sustainability Issues

Learning Objectives

- Become familiar with well-developed and sharply opposed points of view on sustainability issues
- Develop ability to apply critical thinking skills to the opinions of others
- Develop ability to challenge widely held beliefs and form independent judgments
- Develop an appreciation for the nature and value of evidence in forming an opinion
- Promote personal growth by framing important issues that question assumptions and belief systems

Introduction to Debate as a Learning Tool

Debate, sometimes known as forensics, is a powerful learning tool because it gives us a means to reason our ways through difficult, complex issues. Sustainability certainly fits into that category. It is widely considered an area both ambiguous and controversial. For evidence of this, think about the present controversy about global warming, whose very existence is challenged, despite the scientific evidence. Even those who advocate for more responsible concern for the environment often do not agree on the meaning of what "sustainability" is all about. Is it an adjective—for example, we favor sustainable development? Or is it a noun—for example, our business model is sustainable? The word has become so popular and it has been used in so many different contexts that its meaning has become hackneyed. The *Scientific American* decided to explore this topic in greater depth and published a special edition in 2009 entitled, "Top 10 Myths about Sustainability."[1] Among the myths cited were the following:

1. Nobody knows what sustainability really means.
2. Sustainability is all about the environment.
3. Sustainability is too expensive.
4. "Sustainable" is a synonym for "green."
5. New technology is always the answer.

In this complicated, seemingly equivocal context, the debate process helps to build our abilities to express our ideas in the public forum, where advocacy occurs in a democracy.[2] As the leading intellectual Jurgen Habermas noted, public discourse such as debate offers students a chance to call on capitalist society to justify perhaps its weakest points. The German philosopher writes that students have the potential to roll back "colonization of the lifeworld" by encouraging public discussion of critical social issues.[3]

To be able to contribute to the development of solutions that are the core challenges of sustainability, we need the ability to see and understand the world differently than we have been conditioned to see and understand it, that is, to re-vision our world.[4] Re-visioning is a meta-capability, a way of thinking that enables us to function successfully in new and unknown situations and to integrate new understandings with our existing skills and knowledge, leading to a more complex grasp of the issues. Re-visioning increases our ability to handle cognitive complexity.

Thus, the debate format offers a great way to build critical and reflective thinking skills, encourage re-visioning, build cognitive complexity, buttress communication skills, build research skills, both primary and secondary, and review concepts relevant to current issues in sustainability, as well as help us become more resilient. We recommend and rely on debate as a learning tool. Exhibit 3.1 describes the most significant specific skills debate helps to develop.

In this chapter we collect arguments on seven issues related to sustainability in the business environment. Our goal is to present opposing points of view on the same subject. By juxtaposing these opposing points of view, you are encouraged to think critically about them, to explore the author's grasp of the issue, to understand the evidence that is presented to support each point of view, and the assumptions—both implicit and

Exhibit 3.1. Debate as a Learning Tool[5]

Characteristic and skill	Debate format helps develop
• Cognitive complexity	• Argumentation • Respect for integrity of evidence • Integration of knowledge and multiple perspectives • Creation of new patterns of knowledge
• Critical thinking	• Respect for reasoned discourse • Identification of arguments • Test of reasoning (fallacies) • Evaluation of evidence
• Reflective thinking	• Understanding of how others think • Ease with uncertainty • Critical listening skills • Formation of arguments
• Resilience	• Courage • Self-confidence • Acceptance of conceptual conflict • Ease with uncertainty • Social maturity • Persistence • Decision making under pressure

explicit—that are used to frame the argument. Depending on the context, you may be either persuaded or induced to form a personal opinion about the topic. In this Internet-driven age when digital information is so readily available, even if it is not correct, you are now asked to evaluate two diametrically opposed opinions. Which one do you choose? And why? These questions are the subject matter of this chapter.

Opposing Beliefs on Sustainability Issues

Each of seven sustainability issues is presented with two opposing, short essays, followed by some suggested follow-up questions. The seven issues are stated below and, at the conclusion of this chapter, linked to the chapter's five myths about sustainability

1. Is sustainability a realistic objective for society?
2. Should ecosystem services be monetized?
3. Are market-based systems better than government regulations in achieving sustainability?

4. Does geo-engineering offer a sound approach to address climate change?
5. Should water be privatized?
6. Is shale gas the answer to U.S. energy independence?
7. Is the precautionary principle a sound approach to risk analysis?

Issue 1: Is Sustainability a Realistic Objective for Society?

The YES proposition: Sustainability is a realistic objective for society—but we need to make a few changes.

If sustainability means meeting the needs of the present generation without compromising the ability of future generations to meet their needs, as per the definition expressed by the Brundtland Commission,[6] then sustainability is not only a noble goal, it is a necessity. The most basic argument for this position is a simple one, what choice do we have? According to a recent U.N. report, the world population growth rate must slow down significantly to avoid reaching unsustainable levels.[7] If we continue on our present course, future generations will inherit a reduced quality of life that may well include a further degraded ecological environment, a global warming trend that has become irreversible, and political discord based on those increasingly few who have access to what will be thought of as profligate consumption and those pushed closer to survival.

Yet our technologically-advanced economic system is structured to depend on consumption of goods and services. Since the end of World War II, that consumption has been gradually stimulated by two design elements: the concept of fast-changing fashion and the incorporation of planned obsolescence into product design. Both of these approaches to product design imply increasing levels of personal consumption to support corporate and governmental goals for profitability, employment, and economic growth. They would have to change in a sustainable world.

The role of consumption in Western society, especially in North America, has become central to our social life. We tend to equate economic well-being with happiness. No longer are we "keeping up with the Joneses;" shopping now functions as a central social activity. People go to the malls in their spare time; they cruise the stores and look for enticements to consume. We self-actualize through consumption, thanks to the brilliant marketing phenomenon of branding. With fashion-based obsolescence, consumption is pushed into a seasonal structure, and many of us replace last year's coats, sweaters, and dresses with the latest trends, while our cast-off clothing finds its way to second hand and thrift stores. Fashion consumption is tinged with a competitive approach as well: the brand marker of our shirt, shoes, boots, or handbag allows us to assert our status and classify one another in an economic hierarchy. Let's take a look at recent yoga fashion rage. First there was the perfectly functional athletic wear produced locally or by companies such as Rockport, Nike, and Danskin. Then the women's athletic fashion segment arrived, and companies such as Title 9 and Athleta came along. Then the narrower segment of yoga fashion arrived—Lulu Lemon, Hind, Lucy, and Hyde. At each step in the evolution of this category, many of us found our tee shirts too pedestrian for yoga and traded up. Well, we didn't trade, exactly. We donated our "dated" yet perfectly functional yoga gear and bought new ones. Such fashion statements identify us and, paradoxically, contribute to the continuation of a spiritual void, an emptiness in our lives we seek to fill by our practice of yoga. With fashion-based obsolescence, the richness of our individual humanity is reduced to Gucci and Polo, Abercrombie & Fitch, and Water Girl. This fashion-based consumption trend is not good for us and certainly not good for sustainability.

For society to embrace sustainability, we need to address the second design element as well—planned obsolescence that is incorporated into product design. Think about an appliance or piece of equipment that no longer functions properly. Is it better to repair it or replace it? With many technology-based appliances (audio equipment, computer components), we simply replace it. Many of us would not even know where to begin to find someone to repair a non-functioning DVD player. Several businesses are forging the way to produce lasting goods or to re-use their components. The first of these approaches has been taken by Patagonia, the outdoor equipment company begun by the famed climber originally from Maine, Yvonne Choinard. Patagonia will repair any item, usually at no charge. And Patagonia means this, as a repaired rain jacket's zipper, caught in a car door, evidences. Patagonia also has an alliance with eBay, the consumer-to-consumer auction and sales corporation, which is designed to encourage people who have recyclable Patagonia goods that still have utility, to resell them.

At the end of their useful life (which, unfortunately, may not be a long life), the inputs for our discarded CD players, computers, kitchen appliances, and so on, usually enter the waste stream, often adding to pollution. But we can design other approaches to obsolescence. For example, Interface, Inc. is the world's largest manufacturer of the modular carpet, which it markets under several brand names such as InterfaceFLOR. The products are trendy carpet blocks that are designed to be manufactured from recycled and bio-based raw materials, thereby reducing the resources required to make them. This product is especially interesting since the nylon fibers are a petroleum-based product. Ray Anderson, CEO, the founder of Interface, transitioned carpet manufacturing from a petroleum-intensive, high-waste, high energy consumption process into a sustainable process. It took him years, and he kept at it, encouraged by Paul Hawken and others. It can be done! Another approach to obsolescence is for us to demand higher quality goods that last. We don't need new coffee makers every few years if what we have is well-designed, high-quality, and functional. Changing this aspect of our consumption might be psychologically easier than changing our addiction to fashion, and could be done through concerted consumer demand and education.[8]

Both of these impediments to sustainability, our addiction to fashion and our willingness to replace low-quality goods, could be changed, and we would be better both as a society and as individuals if they were. The changes could be consumer stimulated and encouraged by government actions, as well. We can change; we need to change in order to provide future generations with resources similar to those we have. Such changes are the right thing to do and we are capable of doing them. Let's get going.

The NO proposition: Sustainability is not a realistic objective because we resist making changes to our lifestyle.

Our economic system depends on growth, and growth depends on consuming more goods and services. We are by our very nature, consumers. As Americans, we are also inclined to commit to the short term and not take a long-term view of things. This preference for the short term and for acting on rather than thinking through an issue is part of our

American pragmatism: we don't explore and develop the theory. Rather, we get into the situation and face problems as they present themselves to us, with a wonderful on-the-fly adaptability. So the very attributes that a sustainable approach needs—a long-term view and a thoughtful response—are the ones to which we are not especially inclined.

That's the nice way to put it. Others have been more blunt. Sharon Begley, writing in Newsweek, observes that we are ignorant, apathetic, and selfish.[9] She points out that we lack knowledge about how to live in a sustainable way. For example, most people believe that more energy is required to make an aluminum can than a glass bottle. The fact is, using new materials, glass takes 1.4 times more energy, and using recycled materials, glass takes 20 times more energy than does the aluminum can.

Not only is ignorance an insurmountable problem, but so is apathy: we don't care at all about sustainability. Witness the lights left on, the air conditioning system cooling empty rooms in the summer and heating empty rooms in the winter, not to mention the inefficiencies in our nation's transportation system. Individuals in individual cars, most with a gasoline powered engine, consuming fossil fuel, and contributing to global warming through carbon dioxide emissions as they creep along congestion highways during rush hour. Meanwhile, people feel they are promoting sustainability when they turn the abandoned train track into a bike path.

Then there is our basic selfishness. We cannot overcome that. It is part of human nature and arguably the basis of our capitalistic economic system. Actually, a self-centered approach to nature, that it is there for us to master and use, has been argued since 5th century Athens. Domination of nature has led to the assumption that it belongs to us, to use as we want. The idea that we could transition to a new way of thinking about both ourselves and ourselves in relationship to nature has history and current practice against it. So, you see, any movement to sustainability in our lifetimes is hopeless. And that's just the way it is meant to be.

Questions for discussion:

1. Is sustainability a concept that is contrary to human nature? Do we need to accept a lower standard of living to become a sustainable society?

2. If consumers shift their purchasing behavior to buy products that have a long product life and that do not become obsolete quickly, how will this affect economic growth, employment, and foreign trade?

3. What public policies could be created to shift consumer preferences to favor more sustainable product choices? Can you provide examples of existing policies in this regard?

4. What is the role of educational institutions to build a better informed citizenry that is less apathetic about the environment and sustainability?

Issue 2: Should Ecosystem Services be Monetized?

The YES Proposition: The best way to value ecosystem services is to put a monetary value on them.

Ecosystem services refer to the natural processes by which the environment produces resources that we rely on and often take for granted, such as clean water, timber, habitat for fisheries, the decomposition of waste materials, and the pollination of plants.[10] The United Nations formalized this term with its involvement in the Millennium Ecosystem Assessment, a global study of the ecosystem published in 2005,[11] that catalogued and categorized the global ecosystem into four basic groups, by their function: provisioning (such as food, water), supporting (such as pollination), regulating (such as control of climate) and cultural (such as recreation).

Yes, ecosystems have economic value. Although it is difficult to quantify and give a monetary value to everything nature provides, clearly what nature does provide has economic value. One can put a price on these services much like Costanza and his coauthors did in their research, which pegged the value of seventeen specific ecosystem services at $33 trillion dollars per year.[12] Think of the additional costs we would have were clean water not available. No one would argue that ecosystem services have no value; preserving them is what sustainability is all about. The issue is whether we should monetize them, that is, measure their value in economic, monetary terms. How many dollars worth of carbon absorption does an acre of trees produce per year? In order to attach a dollar amount to this service, we will have to measure it. Such an action, despite the estimates involved, will increase awareness of the value of ecosystems and how to protect them. One estimate calculated in 1979 by Costanza and his colleagues put the number at $3.3 trillion annually.[13] That will help overcome one of the major problems with sustainability initiatives, that people are not aware of the impact of their actions. Now, if we know the actual dollar value of the eco-service provided by that forest acre, we are more likely to think more systematically about the impact of clear-cutting the acre, for example. Monetizing the ecosystem services will increase awareness of their value and any actions we take that may affect them.

There are also arguments for monetizing the ecosystem that go to show how assigning dollar values to the ecosystem services could help people build a full understanding of their contribution to our economic lives. That is, we need inputs both from ecologists and economists; otherwise, we will not have a complete picture. With a complete picture, we will be more likely to be able to account for and assess decisions that influence the ecosystem. Over time, is the application of fertilizer to increase crop yield a benefit when compared to the damage of nitrates release into nearby water supplies? Monetizing makes possible an easier linkage between the economic and ecological analysis of ecosystem services.[14]

One main objection to monetizing ecosystem services, as much as doing so makes sense, is that many ecosystem services are public goods that are not traded, so they have no established market value. How do we assign a monetary value to a mountain trail that culminates in a view of other peaks, with cliffs moving toward the ocean? Yet there are ways to approach this valuation challenge, such as utility models and replacement costs.

The NO proposition: Ecosystem services should not be monetized.

Putting a price on nature is troubling, for practical, incompatibility, and philosophical reasons. Some opponents of monetization would add ethical reasons, as well.

Economic value is an important measure in a market economy, which is based on consumption models and resource availability, from plentiful to scarce. Supply and demand are central concepts, and attaching a money value to these consumer items is logical. The problem with this market-based approach to the ecosystem is that the ecosystem is composed of self-sustaining cycles and renewability as normal processes. The bee doesn't engage in a market process as a part of pollination. Water, air, the photosynthesis cycle, all of them occur naturally. Yes, we have built value by harnessing them or their results, such as in agriculture (provisioning) and pollination (supporting). But these natural forces do not form a market. The ecosystem is not about consumption; it is circular and self-renewing.

From a practical perspective, monetizing the ecosystem services is not possible. How do you set a monetary value on photosynthesis or the carbon cycle? OK, we understand that the process would both encounter many methodological problems and depend on estimates. With such a pragmatic approach, by necessity, the estimates would be so broad and thin that they would not be reliable. Understanding how unreliable data would be helpful is difficult. In addition, their unreliability could also cause harm.

Another reason we should not take the path of monetization, tempting as it may be, is that to attempt to monetize ecosystem services could indulge our anthropomorphism and lead us to think that we can control these services and that they are a part of our environment. In actuality, it is we who are a part, however small, of the ecosystem.

Troubling from a philosophical or spiritual perspective is that there are values that many people find in the realm of the ecosystem, that are not monetized. Think of the New England transcendentalists such as Henry David Thoreau, the philosopher of the open air, who found in nature (the ecosystem) an enactment of their spiritual beliefs and philosophical values.[15] In a monetized system, because they cannot be monetized, these human spiritual and philosophical values would become a new endangered species.

Monetization may be useful in some small and limited ways to help us better understand and protect ecosystem services. Yet, we need to be aware of the dangers of monetization and not allow its pragmatic pull to over-simplify the complex workings of nature, including humans. There must be other, less over- simplifying ways to build our understanding of nature and to figure out how to live in it. Thoreau, with his desire to minimize the material world and live simply and fully in the natural one, grappled with the problem of monetizing and concluded that price is directly related to time: "The price of anything is the amount of life you exchange for it." That is to say, the price of the natural world is so elemental that we can measure it only with the time contained in our lives. Dollars miss the mark, totally.

Questions for discussion:

1. In what ways do ecosystems provide valuable services?
2. Is it proper to value an ecosystem service on a single monetary scale?
3. In finance, we use a weighted average cost of capital to evaluate projects whose costs and benefits accrue over time. What is the appropriate discount factor for ecosystem services?
4. Explore the concept of ecosystem services—what they are, why they are important, and how they might be measured.
5. Discuss the advantages and disadvantages of placing a monetary value on our environment.
6. Examine how payments for ecosystem services can help improve the management of natural ecosystems.

Issue 3: Are Market-Based Systems Better Than Government Regulations at Achieving Sustainability?

The YES proposition: Market-based systems are quite efficient and better than government regulations at achieving sustainability.

Environmental policy always provokes a great deal of political rhetoric and debate and it seems to have become more polarized in recent years. No one disputes the major *goals*: we want to live on a planet with clean air, ample supplies of fresh drinking water, land that is not contaminated with toxic materials and food that is nutritious and healthy. We also find common ground on the issue of climate change—we desire living in a world where the rise in temperatures is not causing climate extremes or changes in the sea level. Controversy arises, however, about the primary and secondary causes of environmental problems and, most importantly, on the policy prescriptions and means to achieve these goals.

Economic theory has demonstrated that under certain specific assumptions, the law of supply and demand will influence prices to move to an equilibrium level that balances the demands for the product against the supplies. At the equilibrium price, the market distributes the product to consumers according to each purchaser's preference and within each purchaser's budget constraint. This result is described as being Pareto optimal—no one can be made better off without making someone else worse off. This concept works very well in theory, but the assumptions may not hold up well in practice. The theory assumes the following:

- Producers lack market power.
- Market participants have access to complete information.
- Market participants have free entry and exit.

In actual practice, these assumptions are incorrect. Many industries have few producers, and they have significant pricing power. Also, many markets are characterized by asymmetric information, where one party to a transaction has pertinent information that is not available to others. And many industries have major barriers to entry and exit, such as intellectual property, switching costs, economies of scale, control of critical resources, government regulations, and access to capital.

The divergence between the economic theory of a Pareto optimal society and the real world is no more evident than when we consider environmental policy. Unfortunately, some production processes create costs for people who are not part of the consumption or production activity. These external costs are called negative externalities.

Consider a textile factory that is producing both consumer goods for sale and by-product wastes that are polluting nearby bodies of water. When the factory can dispose of these wastes for free, it has an incentive to dump more waste than is socially optimal. From the firm's perspective, as long as it complies with all applicable laws (and assume for the moment that this includes environmental laws and regulations), then it is following a profit-maximizing strategy. From a societal perspective, however, the textile factory has underinvested in equipment and technology to eliminate the pollutant from the water as it leaves the factory. Its production costs, therefore, are less than what they would have been if their wastes were not harmful, and society's costs are higher. Residents of the area may drink the polluted water, suffer severe health effects, and impose costs on the local health care providers. Neighborhood real estate values may decline, as prospective buyers learn about the poor quality of the drinking water in the area. The municipal water treatment plant may be asked to install specialized, costly equipment to remove the pollutants, resulting in higher local tax levies.

In these situations, the harmful effect of the producer who imposes costs on others—higher health care costs, lower asset values, higher taxes—is a negative externality. To get the perpetrator to pay directly for the harmful effects is difficult, and it is not a simple matter for those suffering the harm to seek an appropriate remedy. The market price for the textile product is set in a competitive market place, and the cost of the externality is not built into this price.

We believe market-based policy instruments can be used to correct market failures caused by under-pricing. With these policies, there is no need for heavy-handed and cumbersome government regulations. We merely need to incorporate the cost of the externality into the price of the product. This can be done in a variety of ways, such as imposing a tax or using tradable permits. In this manner, we can continue to enjoy the benefits of a free market system with only minimal government involvement.

Although no one enjoys paying taxes, a "green" tax that corrects an obvious market failure has many advantages. First, the tax would apply on the volume of pollution created by the factory, and the tax rate should be set high enough to incentivize the producer to reduce the quantity of pollution. Producers will evaluate new technologies and capital improvement projects that mitigate or eliminate the pollution, and the increased costs will be reflected in the producers' prices. Some clever producers might even discover innovative ways to eliminate the pollution altogether and thereby avoid the tax. This would give them a clear competitive advantage. Consumers will compare the variety of products in the market place and make their purchase decisions based on product performance and cost—only now the cost reflects the full cost, including the cost of the externality.

Market-based policy instruments like "green" taxes have many advantages. They are flexible, since the tax rate can be adjusted as often as necessary to provide effective incentives for producers to reduce or eliminate pollution. Taxes also have relatively low compliance costs. One merely has to measure the volume of pollution and multiply that by the tax rate. Routine audits are necessary to assure tax collections. Revenue from the tax can be used to offset other taxes, or it can be rebated to consumers through revenue recycling. In a perfect world, the tax revenue will disappear when the pollution disappears. After all, this was the objective in the first place—a pollution-free planet.

The NO proposition: Market-based systems are not better than government regulations at achieving sustainability.

Market-based systems and "green" taxes may sound good in theory, but often they are not effective in practice. If the tax rate is set too low, producers will not make the necessary changes to production processes to reduce pollution. If the tax rate is set too high, it may be necessary to shut the factory and lay off workers. In addition, domestic producers may suffer a significant loss in market share, since foreign producers are not subject to these "green" taxes. In the rate setting process, a concentrated group of producers will generally apply strong political pressure to set a low rate, provide exemptions for certain transactions such as exports, and thus mitigate the effect of the tax.

We cannot depend on the vagaries of the market to correct these environmental market failures. Direct and targeted regulation that clearly defines the rules of what activities are allowed and what activities are not allowed is necessary. Standards of performance need to be established through a deliberative process that weights the benefits of a pollution-free world against the costs, using a variety of existing and potential technologies. These performance standards can change over time as new technologies are brought to market allowing for higher levels of environmental performance to be achieved.

Direct regulation and setting standards are not sufficient to protect the environment. We must also establish an enforcement mechanism to insure that producers live up to those standards fully. Failure to comply with the standards should result in sanctions and penalties that are defined in advance and severe enough to be an effective deterrent to bad behavior. There are many examples where this approach to correcting market failures has been successful. Take the simple case of wearing seat belts, a safety feature in automobiles that saves lives and lowers overall health care costs for society. Is there a market mechanism that could replace direct regulation? Probably not.

To cite another example, evidence was mounting in the 1980s that chlorofluorocarbons (CFCs) released into the atmosphere were destroying the ozone layer. If left unchecked, higher levels of ultraviolet radiation from the sun would result in millions of Americans developing skin cancer, severe damage to crops and aquatic life, and trillions of dollars in increased health care costs. To complicate the problem, the depletion of the ozone layer is an international environmental issue—no single country acting alone could solve it. Most industrialized countries of the world came together and developed an international treaty, the Montreal Protocol, which established explicit limits on production and consumption levels and a twelve-year phase down schedule. Though there were few available substitutes at the time, producers accelerated research efforts on CFC substitutes, and the phase down schedule was subsequently reduced to ten years. It would be difficult to imagine and more difficult to administer a market based approach that would have been effective as quickly as the Montreal Protocol. As Mario Molina, whose work on CFCs in the atmosphere earned him a Nobel Prize in chemistry, wrote on the 25th anniversary of the Protocol, "This is a planet-saving treaty, protecting both the ozone layer and the climate system."[16]

Government regulations are better than market based approaches to achieve sustainability when urgent action is required to solve pressing environmental problems. The regulations impose fixed standards of performance and impose sanctions on violators. They need not stifle innovation, as demonstrated in the case of the Montreal Protocol. Unlike market based approaches, government regulations can be crafted swiftly and provide certainty to both producers and consumers. Government regulation is a more efficient and targeted approach to achieve the goals of sustainability.

Questions for discussion:

1. Are market-based systems easier to implement than command and control based policies? Why or why not?
2. What are the political ramifications of each type of system?
3. What are the international effects of market-based systems? What are some approaches to mitigate these international effects?

Issue 4: Does Geo-engineering Offer a Sound Approach to Climate Change?

The YES proposition: Geo-engineering offers a sound approach to climate change.

We all realize that climate change is an issue that needs to be addressed. At present there are three general ways of thinking about our approach to climate change: mitigation, adaptation, and geo-engineering.

Mitigation involves the reductions of emissions, essentially undoing the effects of global warming. Within the United States, the world's second largest emitter of greenhouse gases behind China, the political environment has been unfavorable to developing a comprehensive strategy for addressing climate change through mitigation. The primary point of contention centers on the perceived trade-off between economic growth and reduced emissions. Mitigation also has encountered political difficulties, especially between developed and emerging economies.

Adaptation accepts global warming as a *fait accompli* and aims to better position societies and economies to deal with the associated impacts. Like mitigation, adaptation has encountered political and funding challenges, because such funding would be moving wealth from developed to developing economies.

The third approach is geo-engineering, a hybrid and innovative approach to address climate change that involves aspects of both mitigation and adaptation. Geo-engineering is a term that describes an "array of technologies that aim, through large-scale and deliberate modifications of the earth's energy balance, to reduce temperature and counteract anthropogenic climate change."[17] We highlight two geo-engineering technologies for further consideration:

- **Iron fertilization.** Higher iron levels in the world's oceans will stimulate phytoplankton blooms that would capture large volumes of atmospheric carbon dioxide. As the biomass sank, it would take with it the carbon, which would be sequestered deep below the ocean surface.
- **Sulfur reflection.** Scientists believe that sulfur particles or sulfur aerosols placed into the stratosphere will reflect solar radiation back into space and thereby cool the earth's surface. This technique is a form of solar radiation management, or SRM.

Although decarbonization techniques may be part of either a reduction or geo-engineering strategy, SRM includes cloud modification, sun-shading, and sulfur reflection. Cloud modification could involve reducing cirrus clouds, which tend to allow solar radiation through while reflecting infra-red energy back onto the Earth, or marine brightening, where sea spray is employed to make clouds whiter and thus more reflective. Sun-shading uses large mirrors or dust placed in space in such a way that less solar radiation would reach Earth. Sulfur particles may be placed into the stratosphere as a way to reflect solar radiation back into space, or sulfur aerosols could be injected into the stratosphere. The fine particles would then reflect back a portion of the sun's radiation, thus cooling the Earth.

The projected warming in current forecasts is far greater than that of previous forecasts. We know that the reduction approach to climate change is inadequate and its potential effects cannot be offset sufficiently by adaptation. This is largely due to the increasing pace of economic growth—hence, carbon emissions—in the developing world, and the political realities of climate change policy. There is no option on the table other than exploring geo-engineering alternatives, in addition to mitigation and adaptation. Geo-engineering has the potential to augment reduction efforts, not replace them. Although there should be significant effort made to understand all of the implications of geo-engineering, with the potential impact of global warming being as severe as it is, all options must be implemented.[18]

SRM via sulfur aerosols would result in global cooling, at least in the short-term. We have ample evidence for the effectiveness of this approach, as we have watched decreasing global temperatures in the wake of volcanic eruptions. Iron fertilization is supported by less certain evidence presently. But, at the very least, the potential of iron fertilization merits further study as part of a possible comprehensive solution to global climate change.

Paul Crutzen, winner of the Nobel Prize for his work on ozone depletion, has argued that the political realities of climate change mandate that geo-engineering possibilities must be pursued. "By far the preferred way to resolve the policy makers' dilemma is to lower emissions of the greenhouse gases. However, so far, attempts in that direction have been grossly unsuccessful. . . . Therefore, although by far not the best solution, the usefulness of artificially . . . cooling [the] climate by adding sunlight reflecting aerosol in the stratosphere might again be explored and debated as a way to . . . counteract the climate force of growing CO_2 emissions."[19] A similar argument can be made for ocean fertilization. Although opponents of the process point to the potential for unintended consequence and the precautionary principle in opposing geo-engineering, the severity of global warming makes it increasingly difficult to maintain the precautionary principle as a justification for failing to act. The precautionary principle could, in a twist of the argument that debaters love, be applied as a justification for pursuing geo-engineering, because a policy of non-action can be seen to be harmful, thus requiring opponents of geo-engineering to prove that such non-action is justified. The risks of not pursuing geo-engineering are greater than the risks of pursuing it.

A final argument in favor of geo-engineering is cost-based. Geo-engineering could prove to be a very cost effective method when compared to mitigation and adaptation. The direct costs of SRM could be just a few cents on the dollar when compared to the cost of reducing carbon emissions.[20] Similarly, the cost of iron induced sequestration, $0.30–$1.00 per ton, is substantially less than the $12/ton cost in the world's largest carbon trading scheme, the European Union Emissions Trading Scheme.[21]

The NO proposition: Geo-engineering does not offer a sound approach to climate change.

Although there is no question that the issue of global climate change requires an immediate and significant response, the Earth's oceans and atmosphere are highly complex systems and the uncertainty surrounding geo-engineering is too great to merit its being a viable solution. This uncertainty is based on two concerns: efficacy and unintended consequences. The first element of uncertainty, efficacy, is illustrated by sulfur aerosols. Although their particles do result in global cooling, that effect is short-lived, on the order of weeks or months if injected into lower levels of the atmosphere and years in the upper atmosphere. Furthermore, their efficacy could be undermined by significant challenges to their proper distribution. With iron fertilization, scientists do not have a complete picture of how much carbon dioxide is taken up by an iron-fertilized bloom and how much of it would remain in the ocean. Also, although recent research did suggest the algae bloom would sequester carbon for extended periods of time, issues of efficacy and potentially adverse effects on marine ecosystems were not satisfactorily addressed. With SRM, although the use of sulfur to reflect energy from the sun would be effective in reducing the amount of heat absorbed by the Earth, it does not do anything to address the underlying cause of global warming, the increased levels of greenhouse gases. Were the SRM process to be halted after it has begun, then the even greater levels of greenhouse gases would result in a more rapid increase in temperature than would have occurred in the absence of geo-engineering. This increased rate of warming would make adaptation even more difficult and expensive.

Beyond the issue of efficacy, there is also the potential for unintended consequences. One example is with iron fertilization. Current research concludes, "Given the negative effects of [a by-product of iron fertilization] in coastal food webs, these findings raise serious concern over the net benefit and sustainability of large-scale iron fertilizations."[22] Beyond the by-products associated with increased iron levels, the more effective the process is in capturing carbon for the atmosphere, the more adverse the potential impact on the chemistry of the deep ocean. Research into the relationship between iron fertilization and acidification of the oceans concluded, "If the amount of net carbon storage in the deep ocean by iron fertilization produces an equivalent amount of emission credits, ocean iron fertilization further acidifies the deep ocean without conferring any chemical benefit to the surface ocean."[23] Meanwhile, increased carbon dioxide levels in the deep ocean result in a decrease in pH levels, and could have an adverse impact on a variety of marine life and pose a threat to the sustainability of the oceanic food chain. Without a reduction in greenhouse emissions, iron fertilization can only harm the balance of the ocean. Furthermore, the expanded blooms could result in the acidification of the deep ocean and in the depletion of its oxygen levels due to its consumption by animals that also consume oxygen.

Research on SRM suggests a number of potential adverse effects, including that increased sulfate levels result in ozone layer depletion,[24] that geo-engineering could bring several approaches into conflict—unintended consequences—that could be damaging, and that the impact of sulfur dioxide injections into the atmosphere could have the potential to disrupt the monsoons in Asia and Africa, and thus, the precipitation necessary to ensure the food supply for billions of people.[25] Whatever the effects of global warming might be, they could not be much worse than the potential effect of this disruption.

In addition, there is the ethical consideration raised by geo-engineering. Is such a significant intervention in the climate, in the natural order of things, ethical? Whether humans should engage in such an active manipulation of the environment is a different question from whether they have the ability to do so. It deserves careful consideration at a global level before we move forward with geo-engineering in such a way that we commit ourselves to it. And that consideration is despite its efficacy.

Questions for discussion:

1. Does the rise in greenhouse gases justify climate intervention via geo-engineering? Is geo-engineering ethical? Given the adverse effects of global warming, do the potential benefits of a more interventionist approach outweigh the risks?
2. When compared to mitigation and adaptation strategies, how prominent a role should geo-engineering play in the response to global warming?
3. Given that the impact of geo-engineering has implications for everyone on the planet, how should this strategy be implemented? What institution should have the authority to deploy the geo-engineering techniques? If certain countries object to using such an approach, how should those objections be addressed?

Issue 5: Should Water Be Privatized?

The YES proposition: Water should be privatized.

Water is a unique resource. It is essential to human life, it is a vital component of our ecosystem, and the amount of fresh water on the planet has been virtually unchanged since prehistoric times. Population growth and economic development are putting strains on water supplies as the demand for fresh water has outstripped population growth over the past century. Additional pressures are being placed on water systems from a variety of sources including urbanization, increased energy production and use, and changing climate conditions. According to a report by the 2030 Water Resources Group, the gap between global water demand and the currently available water supply may be as high as 40% by 2030.[26] Water resources are being stretched to the limit and will ultimately reach crisis proportions unless we increase the productivity of water use and begin to recognize its intrinsic value.

In efficient markets for standardized products, price information reflects the value of the commodity and the competition between rival suppliers. Transparent prices promote efficient trading and resource allocation decisions. Although imbalances between supply and demand may occur on occasion, they are not permanent. If prices increase and remain at a higher level due to soaring demand or restricted supply, some consumers will switch to substitute products and some suppliers will coax additional volume from their operations. These actions will bring supply and demand back into balance. Furthermore, if this situation appears to be long lasting, investment capital will flow to this sector to enable new capacity additions or improved productivity.

Take the example of gasoline. It is an interchangeable, undifferentiated commodity. Price information is transparent, and most people know its price on a daily basis. When gasoline prices rose dramatically in 2007, consumers noticed the impact on their budgets and changed their behavior. We witnessed more ridership of public transportation, more carpooling, fewer trips to the countryside, and increased sales of more fuel-efficient automobiles. Millions of consumers made rational choices to conserve this scarce resource when faced with much higher prices.

Water also is an interchangeable, undifferentiated commodity, but the water market is not structured like other markets. It is a bulk commodity that is heavy relative to its price. One cubic meter of water weighs about a metric ton. The transportation infrastructure is bulky and heavy as well—witness the ductile iron or concrete pipes used in underground water mains. The pricing of water is also unlike the pricing of other natural resources like oil, natural gas, or gold. The price of water is not transparent. Consumers are not generally aware of the price of the water from their municipal water supplier, and prices do not fluctuate on a daily basis.

Pricing does not seem related to scarcity, cost of service, replacement cost, volume of use, or other standard pricing mechanisms, although there are notable exceptions such as in Singapore and Israel. Subsidies are prevalent throughout the industry, resulting in further pricing disparities. We tend to over-consume water because we do not pay the full cost of using it. This may be due to subsidies or because we do not account for all the infrastructure costs associated with delivery of fresh water to consumers.

The country's infrastructure was largely built more than 100 years ago. It is aging, the technology is outdated, and it is largely owned and operated by thousands of small, local monopolies. There are approximately 52,000 independently-run community water systems in the United States. Since most systems are small to mid-sized, they generally lack the economies of scale and scope that would enable them to be efficient. Our archaic water management practices are segregated into multiple systems with drinkable water, waste water, storm water, gray water, and rain water each operating in a separate silo, lacking centralization and integrated resource planning. As a consequence, the water system is cumbersome to manage, difficult to finance, and very inefficient. Estimates of investment required over the next 20 years—to repair, replace, or upgrade these aging facilities, to meet demographic growth, and to meet new water quality standards—are up to $1 trillion.[27] According to the research published by the Johnson Foundation, "we lose some 6 billion gallons of expensive, treated water every day because of leaky and aging pipes—some 14 percent of the nation's daily use."[28]

As things stand now, we need to stop wasting and mismanaging our water systems. Most importantly, we need to address the country's future capital requirements to repair, replace, and upgrade these systems. The root cause of the problem is the price disparity between today's artificial, subsidized prices and the market price of water that reflects its true value. Local water utilities and their publicly-elected officials are ill-equipped to manage these challenges. They prefer to keep prices low for political purposes. These low prices barely cover operating costs, much less than the cost to support long range capital requirements. Furthermore, these water systems often lack access to financial markets to raise the needed long-term investment capital. Given the large number of small and very small publicly-owned water systems, they lack size and scale to hire professionally trained staff to undertake major capital projects. Less than 4% of the roughly 52,000 water systems in the United States have access to the financial markets to issue their own bonds.[29]

We recommend a solution that is consistent with our country's free enterprise system: privatize our water infrastructure. The private sector is fully capable of dealing with these challenges. It is accustomed to dealing with enormous capital requirements, technological and operational synergies, and innovative pricing structures that balance the need to protect certain groups of customers like the poor, while charging higher rates for industrial and commercial customers. We can expect a privatized water system to charge rates that not only cover its costs but also encourage investment, innovation, efficiency, and new technology. At a minimum, the private sector can be expected to increase the productivity of the system by reducing water losses and by encouraging greater conservation. The private sector will undertake the much-needed overhaul of our water infrastructure.

Some might argue that the private sector's profit motive will deny certain population groups access to water resources or that they will engage in price gouging. Others might argue that water resources are part of our national heritage and should never be controlled by private companies that manage and distribute. We maintain that neither of these arguments is valid. The private sector will pay close attention to the cost of service and return on invested capital. The private sector also will invest in new, innovative technologies that will improve productivity. Privatization will encourage a more streamlined industry structure and a search for economies of scale that elude government-owned enterprises. The public interest is not well served by keeping prices below cost and encouraging overconsumption, waste, and underinvestment. With proper government regulation and support, a market-oriented approach can protect the needs at the bottom of the income scale yet also provide safe, reliable, and affordable water resources for all.

The NO proposition: Water should not be privatized.

Water is not like any other commodity. It is fundamental to health and life and it is, therefore, a basic human right. We cannot expect private companies to make important decisions that affect every human being about this basic right. Who should have access to clean water? What price should be charged? These questions are better left to the government sector where duly elected public officials can answer them through a democratic process.

A private company's main interest is the "bottom line." They are responsible to their shareholders, not the general public. They seek to reduce costs to maximize profits, sometimes at the expense of protecting the environment. Furthermore, when water resources are privatized, public control is transferred to a private corporation to manage as it sees fit. We believe that water resources require public oversight to ensure that people come first, not profits. We cannot expect private companies to put the public interest above their self-interest. Privatization is not a viable solution for our deteriorating and aging water infrastructure problems. Water should be equitably priced and accessible for everyone, regardless of income.

One of the main reasons to oppose privatization of water resources is that it will lead to rate increases. Private water companies are businesses like any other business. They deliver high rates of return to their shareholders by charging customers as much as those customers are willing to pay for water. They are not in the business of offering significant discounts based on income or ability to pay, and they are under to no obligation to provide water to consumers who cannot pay their bills. Private companies may be more efficient than government-owned enterprises, but the efficiency gains will be captured by the shareholders and not the public at large, which will be forced to pay higher water bills. Profits from such a valuable resource should accrue to the public and not to shareholders.

There has been a great deal of research on the issue of water privatization. The most succinct conclusion of this research is provided by David Hall and Emanuele Lobina, two water research specialists, who conclude that "the experiment with water privatization has failed."[30] They cite numerous problems with privatization experiments. To summarize the research findings:

- **Privatization can foster corruption.** Water systems are natural monopolies, and the shift from public to private ownership occurs through negotiation between public officials and their private sector counterparts. Widespread cases of corruption have been reported.[31]

- **Privatization can lead to excessive pricing.** As mentioned earlier, private companies will seek to enter the water business only if there is sufficient financial inducement. This generally means that the company requires a high degree of control over the existing price level and future price increases, and an ability to earn a return on the capital investments required to maintain and upgrade the system. Poorly structured contracts and regulations can result in excessive pricing and consumer backlash.

- **Privatization is difficult to reverse.** Once a municipality has privatized its water resources, the contracts are difficult to unravel without a significant financial penalty. In addition, if the private company fails to live up to the terms of the contract, remedies can be complicated and costly. In a recent example, rather than engaging in a protracted legal battle to buy back its water system from a private company, the City of Chattanooga, TN ended its buy-back efforts and agreed to increase its water rates and other fees by 12%. [32]

We cannot depend on the private sector to provide this basic service. Water systems are natural monopolies and these services are provided best by a single government-owned and operated entity. Claims by privatization proponents that service will improve and water rates will fall are illusory. Any gains from greater productivity and higher prices would be captured by the shareholders, not the general public. We should instead strive to make our government-owned and operating systems more efficient and address the mis-pricing issue without opening the Pandora's box of privatization.

Questions for discussion:

1. Why will the issue of water availability be a major challenge for world leaders in the 21st century?
2. Given the significant capital requirements to build and maintain the water infrastructure, can publicly owned and operated water utilities secure the necessary financing to make these investments?
3. Should water be priced at the full cost of production for residential customers? If not, how should it be priced?
4. Should water conservation issues play a bigger role in the debate?

Issue 6: Is Shale Gas the Answer to U.S. Energy Independence?

The YES proposition: Shale gas is the answer to U.S. energy independence.

- A major strategic objective of U.S. energy policy following the OPEC embargoes of the 1970s has been energy independence. In response to the embargoes, U.S. government leaders pursued a wide range of programs designed to achieve greater non-imported energy supply, including subsidies, low-interest loans, tax breaks, and mandates for wind, solar, ethanol, and other alternative energy sources. Until recently, the United States had made only limited progress in realizing this elusive goal. Fortunately, the situation today is quite different. Without any specific government support, corporations and private investors have poured billions of dollars into the development and production of shale gas, the natural gas that is trapped within dense sedimentary rock formations deep below the surface in North America. Because it was considered too costly to develop and recover, shale gas was categorized as a form of "unconventional" gas. Advances in drilling technology, however, have revolutionized the energy exploration industry and led to a boom in shale gas extraction. These advances include:
- **Horizontal drilling.** The ability to drill down and then turn the drill to follow the lateral formation of the rock layer and increase the recovery rate of the gas.
- **Hydraulic fracturing (or fracking).** The technique of injecting at high pressure a mixture of water, sand, and chemicals to fracture the rock formations and allow the trapped natural gas to be released and recovered.

Using these advanced technologies, the United States has the potential to unlock vast amounts of natural gas. Although estimates of the exact amount of shale gas vary significantly, many experts expect that the United States will not run out of natural gas supplies for at least the next 100 years.[33] Over the past decade or so, over 20,000 shale gas wells have been drilled in the United States and 50,000 additional wells are on the drawing boards. Unlike conventional gas wells, shale wells have a relatively short lifespan. Gas production from an individual well typically declines very steeply after the first few years of extraction and then levels off to low, sustained production levels. Consequently, new wells are being drilled on a continual basis to maintain stable production quantities.

Economies of scale and technological advances have reduced the production cost of shale gas to levels that make them now competitive with conventional natural gas production. Both the surge in shale gas production and its promise for future growth have been major contributors to the very low cost of natural gas in the U.S. Crude oil and natural gas are both energy commodities, and their prices should have a high degree of correlation.[34] Historically, the price ratio of oil to natural gas has been relatively stable, except in periods of extreme market disruption. This pattern, however, started to deteriorate after 2009, primarily due to the combination of rising domestic production of shale gas, which depressed natural gas price levels, and geo-political events in the Middle East and Africa, which added a speculative premium to oil prices.[35]

The shale gas boom in energy-rich regions of the country is revolutionizing the U.S. economy. Drilling activity is bringing millions of dollars into communities, state and local governments, and the pockets of landowners who may be located in impoverished areas. Major shale gas plays are occurring in many parts of North America. Names like Marcellus, Bakken, Barnett, Haynesville, and Fayetteville Shale have become household words. The next big boom could be the Monterrey shale formation, which spans 1,750 square miles in southern and central California.

This turnabout is all the more remarkable given past predictions that in the United States and Canada, natural gas production was dwindling and imports of liquefied natural gas would be necessary to satisfy demand. Now the domestic natural gas market is oversupplied, and manufacturing and chemical companies are considering major plant expansions to take advantage of low energy costs and secure domestic supplies.

The U.S. economy stands to benefit in a number of significant ways from these developments:

- **Lower energy costs.** Lower energy and raw material costs will reduce manufacturing costs and save homeowners billions of dollars per year.

- **Greater demand for domestically produced products.**
  The resurgence in domestic manufacturing has benefited U.S.
  companies, particularly in the chemical, metal, and industrial
  sectors.[36]
- **More jobs.** Employment attributed to unconventional oil
  and gas production added 1.7 million jobs in 2012, and is
  expected to grow to approximately 2.5 million jobs in 2015.[37]
- **Government revenue.** In 2012, unconventional oil and
  natural gas economic activity was expected to contribute
  nearly $62 billion is federal, state, and local tax receipts.[38]
- **Balance of payments.** The shift to domestically produced
  oil and gas improved the balance of payments for the United
  States in 2012 by an estimated $75 billion.[39]
- **Geopolitical benefits.** By depending more on domestic
  energy sources and less on unreliable overseas suppliers, the
  United States will gain significant political and economic
  benefits in improved national security, less reliance on military
  muscle in sensitive, energy-rich regions of the world, and
  better relations with foreign powers.

The shale gas revolution is upon us, and its full ramifications are only
beginning to be understood. The economic and political benefits are significant and strategically important on the world stage. Although there
are environmental concerns, the EPA concluded that horizontal drilling
and fracking were environmentally safe practices. The technology works.
We should embrace these opportunities, carefully manage the environmental risks, encourage innovation and engagement with community
stakeholders, and move forward to achieve energy independence.

The NO proposition: Shale gas is not the answer to U.S. energy
independence.

No one doubts the dramatic effects that the country's headlong rush
to exploit the natural gas contained in shale formations have had on the
economy. The surge in gas supplies has lowered the cost of electricity and
industrial feedstocks and increased economic well-being for millions of
consumers. It has even spurred the use of natural gas as a transportation

fuel. Yet the rush to drill many thousands of wells has economic costs and environmental risks that need to be balanced against the benefits. Although the extraction process may have been deemed "safe" by the EPA, there are serious, potentially irreversible threats to the environment because of faulty and improper execution of the drilling and fracking technology. Some of the major problematic issues are highlighted below.

- **Shale gas production can stress existing fresh water supplies.** The amount of water needed to develop a shale gas well is on the order of four million gallons per well, an amount large enough to challenge water supplies and infrastructure in some regions of the country. We need to balance the water needs of shale gas producers with the needs of other water users, such as drinking water for the population, water for wildlife habitat, agriculture needs, and recreation uses, and the needs of industrial users.

- **Shale gas production can pollute surface and groundwater resources.** Fracking fluids consist of various chemical additives that improve the effectiveness of the process. Some of these chemicals are hazardous in sufficient concentrations, and producers have been reluctant to disclose the exact nature of these ingredients. The risk of contamination to surface and groundwater resources can occur in two ways. Some of the water used in hydraulic fracking flows back to the surface. This flowback water has all the ingredients used in the original fracking fluid. The volume of recovery of the water initially injected into the well is about 25%.[40] The rest of the fluid remains absorbed in the shale formation. The second source of contamination is from the naturally occurring water found in shale formations that flows to the surface throughout the life of the well. This is called produced water, and it often has high levels of dissolved solids and minerals, including barium, calcium, iron, and magnesium. This produced water that is collected at the well site must be managed because of its hazardous nature. Some of it is recycled and can be reused on site; some of it must be trucked to remote disposal sites; whereas some is sent to municipal waste water treatment facilities, which are generally not equipped to handle it. Finally, the fracking fluid that is not recovered at the well site can contaminate potable water aquifers. Although the typical depth of shale wells is often thousands of feet below the drinking water aquifers, there is the risk that some of the fluids under high pressure, bubbling up through cracks and fissures, could pollute the aquifer.

There have been numerous incidents of leaks and spills of hazardous drilling fluids around drilling sites. The leaks have occurred in pumps, hoses, pits, and vehicles, and have contaminated local streams and rivers. For example, in the Marcellus region of Pennsylvania, the state department for environmental protection issued about 1,000 violations to shale well operators in 2011, the majority of which were for leaks, spills, and illegal discharges of contaminated water.[41] These incidents have resulted in polluted streams, fish kills, and serious erosion problems.

- **Methane leaks from shale gas activities contribute to global warming.** The proponents of shale gas development often point to the clean burning properties of natural gas compared to coal. Coal is widely used in electric power generation and is a major contributor to green house gas emissions when it is burned. Natural gas is a cleaner burning fuel when used for electric power generation. However, recent research[42] suggests that methane leaks associated with shale gas development are much higher than expected. The leaks occur during upstream activities like well completions and natural gas production and during mid-stream activities like gas processing. Leaks are an important issue because the global warming potential of methane is more than 20 times more powerful that carbon dioxide. These preliminary findings, if confirmed, raise serious questions about the environmental benefits of shale gas as a replacement for dirtier coal.

- **Shale gas production can create seismic risks.** There has been only one case where fracking was found to have caused an earthquake, but there have been another eight cases where wastewater disposal wells have been suspected of inducing seismic activity.[43] The long-term effects of these practices are unknown at this time. Although most experts consider the risk of induced seismic activity to be low, most shale development has occurred in sparsely populated areas, where earthquakes are not common. This is not the case for Monterrey shale in California, which holds significant hydrocarbon reserves in shale formations and where the natural seismic risk is high.

In conclusion, we agree that shale gas development provides the United States with significant economic and strategic benefits. However, shale gas is a fossil fuel, and its supply will not last forever. Furthermore, we argue that the rapid development of this technology exposes the ecosystem to risks that are poorly understood, any damage may be irreversible, and the unintended consequences might be enormous. Rather than to invest in another form of fossil fuel, we should continue to invest in renewable and affordable energy technologies to secure long-lasting energy independence for our country.

Questions for discussion:

1. Do we need energy so badly that we should ignore the environmental risks to water resources and human health?
2. How will ample supplies of cheap natural gas affect development of renewable energy supplies like wind and solar power?
3. How will shale gas development affect the long-term energy strategy of the United States and contribute to national security?

Issue 7: Is the Precautionary Principle a Sound Approach to Risk Analysis?

The YES proposition: The precautionary principle is a sound approach to risk analysis.

Although the precautionary principle has been applied and re-stated in a number of different forums, it lacks a universally accepted definition. Perhaps the most widely cited definition is the 1998 Wingspread Statement on the Precautionary Principle, which states: "when an activity raises threats of harm to human health or the environment, precautionary measures should be taken even if some cause and effect relationships are not fully established scientifically. In this context the proponent of an activity, rather than the public, should bear the burden of proof."[44] Broadly speaking, the principle supports governmental action to limit the use or manufacture of new products even before a scientific consensus is established that they may be harmful. These actions are often invoked in cases when the use of the innovative technology may have substantial and irreversible effects. For example, the European Union has invoked this principle for the regulation of chemicals under its recently enacted Registration, Evaluation, Authorization, and Restriction of Chemicals, or REACH, program. Certain chemical families have the potential to be persistent in the environment, bioaccumulate in the ecosystem, and be toxic to living organisms. Other chemicals may be endocrine disruptors, which could cause reproductive problems in men and women, impaired immune system functioning, various forms of cancer, and brain and behavioral problems. According to the REACH procedures that became effective in 2007, if there is reliable scientific evidence that a chemical might cause damage to human health or the environment, but the extent of the potential damage remains uncertain, regulators are authorized to exercise precaution.[45]

There are many examples of situations in which application of the precautionary principle would have prevented adverse health consequences or damage to the environment. We cite a few well-documented cases:

- Asbestos—ultimately declared a carcinogen
- Benzene—exposure was ultimately tied to leukemia
- DDT—ultimately led to the cause of reproductive disorders in birds
- CFCs—ultimately determined to destroy stratospheric ozone
- Leaded gasoline—ultimately determined to be a neurotoxin with particularly harmful effects to children's IQ levels and the cause of anti-social behavior.

Now these substances have been totally banned in most countries around the world, or at least subjected to other controls on manufacture, exposure, or use. However, these regulatory measures were not taken until *after* the damage was done, because knowledge about the adverse impacts of these chemicals was not available before they were used in large quantities. Given the damage that these products caused to human health and the environment, we argue that society would be better off if these products had been subject to the precautionary principle.

An underlying theme of the principle is that decision making in the face of extreme uncertainty and ignorance requires caution on the part of policy makers and the public. Science can inform a decision, but it is often inadequate to prove cause and effect. Nor can science resolve difficult issues and tradeoffs in the absence of adequate data. Science is also limited in providing guidance when ethical and moral considerations emerge, as for example, with genetically modified foods, cloning, and stem cell research. Modern biology and genetics research has advanced so rapidly that George Church, a genetics professor of the Harvard School of Medicine, stated that it would be possible to clone a Neanderthal baby from ancient DNA if researchers could find a woman willing to act as a surrogate.[46] Because scientists can do incredible things, does that mean they should? Assessing the risk of a novel technology or product is not an easy task, and risk calculations are subject to bias and errors of inadequate scope.

In this context, the precautionary principle distinguishes the two concepts, risk and uncertainty. Unlike uncertainty, risk can be quantified— experiments can be undertaken, various possible outcomes can be defined, and probabilities can be assigned to the outcomes. However, many novel technologies can have unintended consequences. With these new technologies, various possible outcomes can be identified, but probabilities of occurrence cannot be determined with any accuracy or credibility. Yet policymakers still need to make decisions in their regard. Furthermore, some possible outcomes can have long-lasting, enormous, and irreversible consequences, even when their probability of occurrence is small. Under these circumstances, the precautionary principle holds that the burden of proof should fall on the proponents of the activity to demonstrate that it is safe. This is not the traditional approach to environmental regulation, especially in the United States, where the burden for proof that an activity should be regulated is placed on the government. The U.S.

Environmental Protection Agency (EPA) maintains a database of existing chemicals, conducts periodic testing, collects data to manage risks, and takes regulatory action only if necessary. According to the EPA, most new chemicals are approved for use without being restricted or regulated in any way. There are over 80,000 chemicals already in use commercially. Only after a problem occurs does the EPA take action. We need to change this paradigm and shift the burden of proof that an activity is safe to the proponents of the activity, not leave it to the government to prove that an activity is unsafe. After all, it is better to be safe than sorry.

The NO proposition: The precautionary principle is *not* a sound approach to risk analysis.

Our modern, technologically-advanced society is complicated: we live with risks every day. The precautionary principle is a simple, deceptively attractive idea, and it sounds so sensible. After all, we install smoke alarms to warn us of fire hazards in our homes and workplace, we wear seat belts and motorcycle helmets for protection in case of a highway accident, and we tolerate full body scans when we board commercial airliners. Regulators of these activities have determined that the cost of these precautionary actions (installing smoke detectors, wearing seat belts, undergoing transportation security screens) are minor inconveniences compared with the potential consequences in the event of a fire, an automobile accident, or a terrorist attack. We choose to mitigate the problem rather than prohibit the activity entirely. This approach is particularly appropriate if there are no suitable alternatives available that consumers could choose.

In many instances, however, the proponents of the precautionary principle place more emphasis on the potential risks than the potential benefits of an activity. The precautionary principle favors status quo by giving too much weight to anecdotal evidence and other theories of risk to health and the environment. The principle can erroneously magnify the risks of very low-probability occurrences, leading to over-regulation and unwarranted prohibitions or restrictions on potentially beneficial products and technologies. For example, the artificial sweetener saccharine was nearly banned by the Food and Drug Administration. Experimental research found that when mice consumed huge doses of saccharine (equivalent to an adult drinking over 300 glasses of diet soda), they developed bladder cancers. An act of Congress overturned the FDA's ban, and recently saccharine was removed from the official list of carcinogens.[47]

The number of alleged hazards that we are exposed to daily far exceeds the number that can ever be proven by sound science, and the popular press and Internet blogs are filled with unproven claims of danger. Examples include the following:

- The fear that the MMR vaccine (for measles, mumps, and rubella) was linked to autism caused many parents to resist vaccinating their children, putting their own children and the broader community at risk for these diseases.
- The opposition by some experts to fluoridation of the water supply on the grounds that it may cause serious health problems and by other groups who suspect that the practice is a Communist plot to undermine public health.
- The opposition to genetically modified crops in certain parts of the world like the European Union has centered essentially on the limitations of science and the desire for certainty. Since scientific findings are probabilistic in nature and therefore uncertain, the critics of the practice cite the use of precaution against the slight probability of a catastrophic outcome.
- The artificial sweetener cyclamate, unlike saccharine, was officially banned for use in diet food and beverages by the FDA after intense public pressure and mass hysteria. The agency based its decision on limited scientific evidence, which could not be replicated by other scientists. It is stilled banned in the United States, although it is available in 55 other countries.

There is an inherent bias in the precautionary principle that favors status quo over novel technologies and products. The principle focuses exclusively on the downside risks of an activity but largely ignores the activity's potential benefits. Consider the case of genetically modified food. The opponents fear that genetic modification will result in serious ecological damage and dangers to human health such as infertility, immune system problems, and accelerated aging, even if they cannot quantify the downside risks with any precision. Yet genetically modified foods hold out the prospect for significantly higher productivity in agriculture, by providing crops that are less costly and healthier than traditional crops. These benefits are particularly important in the developing world.

An interesting parallel to the precautionary principle comes from the economic and decision theory experiments of Amos Tversky and Daniel Kahneman.[48] They demonstrated a concept called "loss aversion." People dislike losses far more than they like corresponding gains. For example, someone who loses $100 is significantly less satisfied than another person who gains a $100 windfall. In the context of the precautionary principle, out-of-pocket costs or losses from the status quo seems much worse than opportunity costs or benefits foregone.

In conclusion, we argue that there is no substitute for the proper assessment of risk and that there is no better way to inform decision makers than sound science tempered with rational debate. We need to consider and weigh the costs and risks of an activity against the potential benefits and allow for an adequate margin of safety. We realize that people tend to over-react to miniscule risks, and we need a reasoned approach for dealing with this tendency. The application of the precautionary principle also tends to stifle innovation. Thus, we argue that the precautionary principle does not provide a sound basis for risk assessment, and it stifles innovation.

Questions for discussion:

1. Should we pay more attention to the potential risks of an activity or the potential benefits? Defend your answer.
2. How may the application of the precautionary principle set obstacles in the path of developing countries?
3. Describe the relationship between the precautionary principle and scientific evidence.
4. To what extent must the precautionary principle require that all nations respond to environmental problems in the same way?
5. Thinking about the previous six discussion questions, does the precautionary principle change or challenge your assumptions on any of the prior issues?

Issues Linked to Myths

The seven issues we have just explored can be linked to the five sustainability myths *Scientific American* described earlier in this chapter. To review, these myths are:

1. Nobody knows what sustainability really means.
2. Sustainability is all about the environment.
3. Sustainability is too expensive.
4. "Sustainable" is a synonym for "green."
5. New technology is always the answer.

Here is the linkage between the issues and these myths:

1. Is sustainability a realistic objective for society?
   This issue is an example of myth #1—nobody knows what sustainability means.
2. Should ecosystem services be monetized?
   This issue is an example of myth #3—sustainability is too expensive.
3. Are market-based systems better than government regulations in achieving sustainability?
   This issue is a combination of myth #2 and #4—sustainability is all about the environment and is a synonym for green.
4. Does geo-engineering offer a sound approach to address climate change?
   This issue is an example of myth #5—new technology is always the answer.
5. Should water be privatized?
   This issue is an example of myth #3—sustainability is too expensive.
6. Is shale gas the answer to U.S. energy independence?
   This issue is an example of myth #5—new technology is always the answer.
7. Is the precautionary principle a sound approach to risk analysis?
   This issue is a combination of myth #4 and #5—it is a synonym for green and new technology is always the answer.

Summary

In Chapter 3 we have reviewed opposing points of view on seven critical issues at the center of sustainability-related controversies and linked these issues to commonly held myths about sustainability. By juxtaposing these opposing points of view, we encourage you to think critically about them, to explore the authors' motivations and value systems, as well as their grasp of the issues, to understand what evidence is presented to support each point of view, and what assumptions—both implicit and explicit—are used to frame the arguments. The myths should assist this critical thinking process. Depending on the context, you may have been persuaded or induced to form a personal opinion about the topic. Which position do you choose? Why?

Our underlying goal in exploring these complex issues is to help you understand that most of the controversial issues related to sustainability, many of which the public needs to understand so that it can weigh in on the development of policy related to them, are not easily resolved. They are exceedingly complex. There may be no right answer available to us, but rather, better ways to approach the issue's management. We need to build our skills in working with complex thinking and argumentation in order to understand what would constitute the best, not the right, sustainable approach.

CHAPTER 4

Decision Making in Sustainability: Case Studies

Learning Objectives

- Become familiar with some of the basic issues raised in teaching cases across the area of sustainability
- Identify, research and develop solutions to problems raised in cases

We learned in the previous chapters that sustainability in the business context involves complex trade-offs—for example, choosing between short-term costs and long-term benefits or between low-risk established technologies and higher-risk (and perhaps better for the planet) new technologies. In business, the facts and circumstances of any given situation often will differ, depending on the industry, the state of the economy, and the core values of the company and its executives. We live in an ambiguous world. In this context, educators for years have used case study research to highlight real-life situations and present students with the challenge of using a limited number of events or conditions to analyze managerial decisions and develop strategy options. Some case studies ask the reader to make specific recommendations to management—and to support these recommendations with careful and insightful analysis. Other case studies provide useful histories of business issues or relevant background material on particular topics.

In this chapter, we collect and summarize a variety of case studies on sustainability-related topics. Our operational definition of sustainability in making these case choices is to use the triple bottom line approach or, as it is often described, the three P's, the need for companies to balance the *Profit* motive with a desire to safeguard the *Planet* and operate with a concern for *People*—employees, the community, customers, and other stakeholders. These cases illustrate decision making around sustainability issues. For simplicity, we have grouped these cases into six sections, based on their major focus —entrepreneurial business models, the green consumer market, the regulatory environment, consumer pressure for change, the implementation of change in mainstream companies, and sustainability and corporate finance. However, this categorization is one of convenience, and readers may choose to use these cases to achieve many other learning objectives. The cases contained in each section are designed for use in courses in sustainability in the business environment, corporate strategy, finance, marketing, entrepreneurship, business policy, and supply chain management. We summarize the major points in each case to explore the usefulness of the case, and we do not propose any case solutions or how readers might frame a case analysis. Review of this material will also give students a sense of the decision-making context around sustainability issues. Readers interested in learning more about a case can then acquire it from the appropriate source identified in the endnote.

Entrepreneurial Business Models

The cases in this section describe several examples of successful entrepreneurs who have developed new business models that seek to blend market and mission-oriented values and strategies. In these cases, the entrepreneurs followed non-traditional paths to achieve business success. These cases are designed to help the reader evaluate alternative business models, investigate the sustainability issues related to these various markets, and understand that profit maximization is not the only goal of a new business.

Burt's Bees: Leaving the Hive[1]

Summary

This case relates the story of how Roxanne Quimby and Burt Shavitz, the founders of Burt's Bees, grew the company from the back of a pick-up truck selling honey-based products in rural Maine in 1984 to become the leader of natural personal care products. Their original vision was to develop earth-friendly products that would offer superior products at a premium price. They worked hard to create products that were consistent with their mission to offer their customers the "greater good"— their corporate motto. The company's culture and brand exuded an anti-commercial image of friendly quirkiness as exemplified by Burt Shavitz's face on the package. The company was committed to the environment and to using natural ingredients. Burt's Bees defined its products as harvested from nature, meaning that the essential ingredients were derived mostly from plants, fruits, and seeds, and they avoided traditional chemicals and fillers. Unlike most of their competitors in the personal case business, the company used only natural colors and fragrances. The company labeled each of their products with a "natural bar" to inform consumers what percentage of the product was natural, and they used small packages so that consumers would finish the product before its expiration date. In addition, they used packaging from recycled materials. The company attracted employees who generally shared this corporate culture and vision.

As CEO of the company, Quimby was able to achieve significant sales growth over the years, while Shavitz showed less interest in the business and retired to Maine in 1999. Rapid growth in the company was accompanied by management challenges and, in 2003, Quimby sold an 80% interest in Burt's Bees for $180 million to a private equity firm that would continue to grow the firm but allow her to maintain an active role. The private equity firm had a reputation for buying small companies, improving the image and sales, and then either selling them to a strategic buyer or taking them public. Quimby stayed on until 2004, and then John Replogle, an experienced manager from Unilever's North American division, came in as the new CEO. The new team made immediate improvements by streamlining the product line, imposing tighter inventory controls, improving the sales forecasting process, and, overall, by bringing fresh eyes to the business. In 2007, the Clorox Company acquired Burt's Bees. The question remains whether the company can continue to grow and maintain its core values for the greater good. For a short background on the company's founders and its history, see this Internet video: http://www.youtube.com/watch?v=NADaAvW5_4Q

Learning Objectives

This case has been used in courses on Sustainability in the Business Environment, Entrepreneurship, Marketing, and Corporate Strategy. The learning objectives are:

1. Understand how a mission-oriented business can thrive in an entrepreneurial environment.
2. Explore the tension between maintaining a quirky corporate culture in a high growth environment.
3. Examine the issues around the transition from an entrepreneurial manager to a more traditional corporate culture.

Guideline Questions

1. Can Burt's Bees become a mainstream product in the personal care market—similar to Starbucks' position in the coffee market—while remaining true to its core values?
2. Can other companies replicate their "Greater Good" business model?
3. What are the risks and opportunities for Burt's Bees business following acquisition by Clorox?

Social Entrepreneurs: Correcting Market Failures (A)[2]

Summary

When there is a market failure, that is, an inefficiency that results in a lower overall level of economic value or social welfare, the traditional response has been government intervention. Recently a new form of business model has developed in the form of social entrepreneurship. While social entrepreneurs are similar to traditional entrepreneurs in that they begin and manage their own organization using a variety entrepreneurial skills and market principles, they are different in an important way—they prioritize social impact over the creation of wealth. This difference in priorities has enabled social entrepreneurs to develop new ways of creating social value by serving the needs of poor, disadvantaged, and neglected communities.

The case presents the backgrounds and business models of three social entrepreneurs. David Green of Project Impact was a forensic cost accountant by training. He developed an innovative approach to manufacturing low-cost, high quality medical supplies to treat and prevent blindness and deafness in the developing world. Green's approach focused on eliminating the price disparity (not income disparity) that kept basic goods and services out of reach of the poor. Victoria Hale of OneWorld Health worked for the U.S. Food and Drug Administration and was a pharmaceutical scientist. She sought to develop new medicines for the infectious diseases that killed millions of people in the poorest parts of the world. Hale sought to correct the issue of promising drugs being abandoned by Western pharmaceutical companies because they were not sufficiently lucrative. Jim Fruchterman of Benetech was an engineer by training and a successful Silicon Valley entrepreneur. Using a venture capital approach to start new businesses, he created technology-based projects that ranged from reading machines for the blind to innovative software to protect both information and the people who collect it in the human rights field. Fruchterman brought a variety of useful technologies to the social sector, which had been dismissed as insufficiently profitable. For a short description of Jim Fruchterman's evolution to become a social entrepreneur, take a look at the Internet video: http://www.youtube.com/watch?v=4UMhTbkZYWg

Learning Objectives

These cases have been used in courses on Sustainability in the Business Environment, Business Ethics, Corporate Social Responsibility, Business and the Developing World, Economic Development, and Innovation. The learning objectives are:

1. Understand what motivates social entrepreneurs and how they differ from traditional entrepreneurs.
2. Become aware of some of the ways in which market failures can arise and the variety of ways in which those failures can be addressed without government intervention.
3. Understand the skills and experience that a group of social entrepreneurs drew on to launch their own enterprises.

Guideline Questions

1. What specific personal skills did Green, Hale, and Fruchterman have that led to their success as social entrepreneurs?
2. Identify the market failures faced by each entrepreneur and compare/contrast their approaches to correcting the market failures. What were the key success factors for each entrepreneur?
3. What general recommendations could you make to the three regarding these issues?
4. Can the social entrepreneurship business model be applied to non-medical market failures without direct government action?

Tapping the "Green" Consumer Market

The cases in this section describe how some companies have succeeded in developing new products to meet increasing consumer demand for more sustainable products. In some cases, the company's original intent was to tap this market segment. In other cases, the company had to change its processes and practices to reach this target market. These cases are designed as an opportunity for the reader to evaluate the challenges for an established company that may be associated with unsustainable or hazardous materials. They present the opportunity to think about how a company can try to rebrand itself to capture a larger slice of the growing "green" consumer market.

Cradle to Cradle Design at Herman Miller: Moving Toward Environmental Sustainability [3]

Summary

Having adopted the triple bottom line approach of measuring performance in financial, environmental, and social responsibility terms, furniture designer Herman Miller adopted a cradle-to-cradle (C2C) design protocol that emphasized environmental sustainability. Implementing the C2C protocol required not only a commitment by senior management to the decision-making process but also a significant commitment of staff time and money. Their goal was to create a zero-waste product where all the materials could be re-used and remain in a closed loop. Zero waste would allow the company to eliminate the adverse effects of the product's disposal in landfills or other harmful means of disposal. The company chose this protocol to design its new mid-level office chair, the Mirra chair. The C2C process, however, was not without trade-offs and risks—technical, financial, and market. The central decision in the case was the choice of two different plastic materials in the arm pad of the new chair. The material usually chosen for the application was polyvinyl chloride (PVC), widely used throughout the industry and not very costly. The potential replacement plastic was thermoplastic polyurethane (TPU), more environmentally friendly but more costly. In addition to the cost issue, choosing TPU would introduce technical risks, since the engineers at Herman Miller were not familiar with this material. It could also present timing issues if the production schedule could not be met. There were quality and performance differences between PVC and TPU that had to be weighed. Using TPU, however, could provide the company with potential first-mover marketing advantages by offering customers a PVC-free chair developed with the C2C design protocol.

The tactical issues of implementing the C2C design protocol presented one set of challenges—whether to choose PVC or TPU. On another level, the case also raised some important strategic issues. Should Herman Miller try to capture the value created by the new protocol? Although the firm desired to be environmentally responsible, much if not all of the value derived from the C2C protocol would be captured not by the firm, but by society. Yet successful implementation of this strategic initiative would enable the company to be an environmental and product design leader in the office furniture industry and provide marketing and public relations benefits. As the first to adopt the C2C protocol and its higher performance standards, Herman Miller could hope to enjoy increased influence in legislation and public opinion in a way that could then, over time, result in a competitive advantage. It is in this way that the furniture designer would be able to capture the value of its initiative. While C2C imposed upon the company an immediate cost, it offered a potentially significant long-term benefit. For background on William McDonough's description of C2C design, take a look at the Internet video: http://www.ted.com/talks/william_mcdonough_on_cradle_to_cradle_design.html

Learning Objectives

The case has been taught in courses on Sustainability in the Business Environment, Marketing and Innovation, Operations Strategy, and Environmental Management. The learning objectives are:

1. Introduce readers to the C2C design protocol—how it works, what the challenges of implementing it are, and what some of its benefits are.
2. Explore the tension between implementing a far-ranging environmental initiative and the practical aspects of its implementation in day-to-day operations.
3. Understand how the creation of a strategic vision imposes behavioral changes throughout the organization and the company's relationships with its suppliers.
4. Show how a firm can capture first-mover strategic advantage from an environmental initiative.

Guideline Questions

1. How did Herman Miller implement the elements of the C2C design protocol for the Mirra chair? How does this implementation plan differ from the traditional plan?
2. Why was the C2C design protocol so resource intensive and expensive?
3. What factors should be considered in making the decision to use PVC or TPU for the Mirra chair?
4. What is your recommendation, choosing between PVC and TPU?
5. Why did Herman Miller make this strategic environmental initiative such a high priority?

Clorox Goes Green[4]

Summary

Clorox is a well-known manufacturer of household consumer products including laundry additives and bleach, home and institutional cleaning products, and water filtration systems. Their flagship product, Clorox

Bleach, represents about 13% of company sales, and the company holds the number one or number two market share position for most of its brands. Clorox cleaning products contain chemicals that have adverse health effects if improperly exposed, and the company's branded products are not considered "green." In fact, Clorox and other industry leaders in household consumer products ignored the green products industry throughout the 1990s. Clorox's major customers were big-box stores such as Walmart, Target, and Costco. Meanwhile, a number of smaller, entrepreneurial companies such as Seventh Generation and Method Products introduced green cleaning products as early as 1987. These companies captured consumers in increasing numbers, particularly among the more educated and those willing to pay a price premium consistent with their lifestyle. However, in much of the 1990s, green cleaning products were considered inferior and overpriced.

In the mid-2000s, as growth in traditional markets slowed, Clorox began to focus on new product innovation as the source for future market success. The green industry had improved product performance, and, with a change in senior management, Clorox decided to develop its own line of environmentally-sensitive products. The target market segment was the "Chemical Avoiding Natural" group of consumers. This group wanted greener cleaning products but felt that the presently available products did not perform well, came from unknown or un-trusted brands, were too expensive, or not available where they shopped.

In 2008, Clorox announced the launch of GreenWorks, a line of naturally sourced cleaning products developed through internal R&D efforts. These products did not compromise on performance, and Clorox priced them 10%–20% above traditional cleaning products. Clorox even disclosed the ingredients in GreenWorks, a significant departure from established company norms. To boost the company's marketing campaign, Clorox established a partnership with the Sierra Club, which endorsed the product line in exchange for a share of the profits. This proved to be a controversial strategy for both Clorox and the Sierra Club. When Green-Works products came to the shelves in 2008, sales exceeded expectations and quickly captured 40% of the market for green cleaning products. Will the success of GreenWorks provide a halo effect for the rest of Clorox? Will there be a competitive reaction from the green market segment and from the traditional competitors? What new opportunities to leverage the success of GreenWorks should Clorox consider? These and other issues are raised in the case. For a brief background on GreenWorks, take a look at the following video: http://www.youtube.com/watch?v=S8FRatAJsB8

Learning Objectives

The case has been used in courses on Sustainability in the Business Environment, Corporate Strategy, Entrepreneurship and Innovation, and Environmental Management. The learning objectives are:

1. Explore the challenges of introducing a line of new products (green products) that are perceived by the market place as dissimilar to the company's established brand (harsh chemicals).
2. Explore the tension in switching strategies from fast follower to first mover.
3. Show how a firm can capture strategic advantage by taking an environmental initiative.

Guideline Questions

1. What factors went into the decision to (a) invest in R&D to develop a new brand, (b) make an acquisition, or (c) extend its existing product line?
2. What was Clorox's pricing strategy for GreenWorks and what factors contributed to its success?
3. Can Clorox leverage the success of GreenWorks in other areas? If so, how?
4. What are Clorox's next strategic moves in the green marketplace?

Whole Foods Market, Inc.[5]

Summary

Whole Foods started as a single food store in 1980 and by 2006 had grown to become the leading natural foods retailer in the United States and the country's fastest growing grocery chain. The competitive landscape was shifting from small independent natural and organic food outlets to major traditional food chains and big discounters like Walmart.

The case describes Whole Foods' history and culture, showing how it developed its strategy and built a structure that allowed rapid adaptation to local market conditions. John Mackey, the founder, began his career as part of an organic food co-op but soon expanded the scope of his business to include a wider range of "natural" products. Along the way, the company established its own retail brand as its fortunes rose on the natural food trend. Whole Foods achieved its rapid expansion by opening new stores in strategic locations and acquiring small, regional "niche" competitors in new territories. One of its key core competencies was its expertise in managing fresh meat, fish, and produce, which attracted customers to shop more often at Whole Foods. A bright and pleasant store atmosphere, the ability to sample foods, and seating areas for people to eat and meet friends encouraged customers to visit and spend more money. The company was able to achieve high levels of worker productivity by motivating teams of employees and by encouraging greater employee retention. Furthermore, Whole Foods was successful in charging a significant price premium, which enabled it to earn profit margins higher than the industry average.

Success breeds imitation, however, and Whole Foods is facing competitive threats from direct rivals like Wild Oats Markets, Inc. and mass merchandisers like Walmart, who want a bigger slice of the natural foods market place. John Mackey is contemplating the rapid expansion of his business in organic foods to natural foods. Not only is he facing serious competitive pressures, he is also dealing with issues such as the tradeoff between environmental objectives and traditional shareholder value imperatives. For a short interview with John Mackey, take a look at the following video: http://www.youtube.com/watch?v=ym-OusRtcoI

Learning Objectives

The case has been used in courses on Sustainability in the Business Environment, Corporate Strategy, Marketing, and Entrepreneurship and Innovation. The learning objectives are:

1. Explore how business strategy evolves over time.
2. Show how a firm can capture strategic advantage by capitalizing on a trend toward a healthier life style.
3. Explore the strategic options of competing against much larger rival firms and the use of agility as a competitive advantage.

Guideline Questions

1. What is the definition of "natural foods?" How does it differ from other concepts like organic, fair trade, or sustainably grown food?
2. What makes the natural food market an attractive business opportunity?
3. What was Whole Foods' business strategy in its early years, and how did it change over time?
4. What are the major threats to Whole Foods' leadership position in the natural foods industry? What can Whole Foods do to maintain its leadership position?

Sustainability and the Regulatory Environment

The cases in this section assess the ways in which government regulation of environmental issues alters markets, industry structure, and business strategy. The regulations often are shaped to address market failures or situations where free markets fail to allocate resources efficiently. This group of cases is designed to analyze the complexities of policy decisions and explore how environmental regulations impact a business, sometimes as a constraint on their practices and sometimes as a business opportunity.

Du Pont Freon Products Division (A)[6]

Summary

The case of the Du Pont Freon˚ products division highlights how the forces of scientific discovery, competitive markets, and national and international regulation can influence corporate strategy and environmental sustainability. The Freon˚ products division manufactured chlorofluorocarbons (CFCs), a group of highly engineered chemical compounds used principally in refrigeration, solvents, foam blowing, aerosol propellants, and fire extinguishing. CFCs had been invented by Du Pont in the 1930s, and the company reaped significant early rewards because these products were inherently safe for use. They were chemically stable, low in toxicity, and non-flammable. By the late 1980s, the division generated sales of about $600 million dollars annually and was the world leader in innovation, research, and development. Du Pont also enjoyed strong customer loyalty.

In 1972, two chemists first postulated a link between CFCs and the depletion of the ozone layer, and in 1978, the U.S. government took action that restricted their use as aerosol propellants because that application was deemed a non-essential use. Du Pont then opposed further regulation or restrictions on the use of CFCs, claiming that the scientific case against CFCs was inconclusive. However, evidence supporting the link continued to mount throughout the 1980s. Member governments of the United Nations began to negotiate severe restrictions on CFCs that would clearly affect Du Pont's business prospects. In September 1987, an international accord, the Montreal Protocol, held each country to its 1986 levels of CFCs and promised to cut CFC production in half by 1989. A video that explains the research on ozone depletion in 1987 can be viewed at: http://www.youtube.com/watch?v=BiGX0V3u4XU

The setting for the case is 1988. Facing these severe external pressures, Du Pont decided that it needed to respond by developing appropriate strategy options. The Montreal Protocol represented a challenge to Du Pont's existing division. It also represented an opportunity for Du Pont to dramatically ramp up research on CFC substitutes, establish a significant market share for these products, and enhance its leadership role within the industry. There were also significant risks associated with each strategy option from a profit, corporate culture, and public relations perspective, as well as risks regarding future scientific findings and persistent scientific uncertainties. In this highly-charged atmosphere, Du Pont had to make critical decisions about its strategy going forward.

Learning Objectives

The case has been taught in courses on Regulation, Sustainability in the Business Environment, Environmental Management, and Strategy. The learning objectives are:

1. Explore the strategy options for a firm when the demand, supply, and competitive conditions have been dramatically altered in a highly charged political situation.
2. Understand how companies can respond when scientific findings—even those that have not yet been proven—create political and regulatory pressures for change.
3. Examine the nature of externalities and public goods in the context of business-government relations.

Guideline Questions

1. Considering the market for CFCs in North America and Europe, how will the Montreal Protocol affect the market structure, production and consumption volumes, and prices in each region?
2. How will the Montreal Protocol affect the political landscape and regulatory climate for CFC producers like Du Pont?
3. What are the strengths and weaknesses of Du Pont's CFC business in 1986?
4. What are the strategy options for Joe Glas, the CFC business manager, moving forward? Which of these options do you recommend?

Molten Metal Technology (A)[7] and (B)[8]

Summary

The Molten Metal Technology (MMT) cases provide some interesting lessons in the challenges and pitfalls of building a dynamic high-tech environmental remediation and services company from scratch. In Case A, which covers the 1989–1995 period, the story unfolds like a fairy tale. A young PhD graduate student at MIT, Christopher Nagel, performed research on a new process to treat hazardous wastes by dissolving them in a bath of molten metal. The high temperature metal bath breaks the chemical bonds of the hazardous chemicals so that the constituent elements can be largely reformed into re-usable commercial products or benign by-products. A video, *Molten Metal Technology—Elemental Recycling: The Future of Environmental Technology*, explains the process quite simply (http://www.youtube.com/watch?v=kg1EaEGXdoI).

Since the process worked successfully in the laboratory, Nagel applied for and received a patent on the process, called the catalytic extraction process (CEP), with the intention of commercializing it. He then teamed with William Haney, a 27-year old entrepreneur from Harvard, who had already started and sold a company that earned him millions of dollars. MMT was formed in 1989 with Haney as CEO and Nagel as chief scientist. The next 6 years saw a fairly continuous stream of business successes and public accolades. CEP was hailed as the technology of the future in the waste management industry, replacing conventional disposal methods such as incineration. Success was fueled by the energetic management team, which garnered lucrative government contracts and established strategic partnerships with leading global corporations like Fluor Daniel, Du Pont, Westinghouse, Rollins Environmental, and Lockheed Martin. In addition, the regulatory climate was favorable to novel, environmentally attractive technologies like CEP. Furthermore, the general population was becoming increasingly aware of the need to safely dispose of hazardous waste streams. The U.S. Congressional Superfund Amendments and Reauthorization Act of 1986 significantly raised the cleanup standards for polluted manufacturing and landfill sites and heightened interest in game-changing remediation technologies such as CEP. Unlike competing technologies, which often only tried to stabilize hazardous waste streams, CEP promised their simple destruction and an opportunity to re-use and re-sell the resulting by-products. Politicians, including Al Gore, embraced MMT and praised its business mission, and the company received endorsements and interest from eminent scientists, public officials, regulators, and potential investors. The stars seemed so perfectly aligned that in 1993 the company issued stock through an Initial Public Offering that raised a fresh $80 million.

From 1993 to 1996, the company continued to expand for the purpose of demonstrating the economic and technical viability of the CEP process with a wide variety of process streams and operating conditions over long periods of time. The leap from success in the laboratory to full commercialization is not an easy one. Yet the company earned its first profit in 1995 and some independent financial analysts recommended MMT as a "strong buy" to investment clients. However, other advisors warned that, although the technology had potential, the financial risks were still too high to justify the lofty $500 million market capitalization.

The MMT Case (B) follows the company over the period 1996 to 1997. Despite the rosy financial predictions and Haney's success in securing lucrative government contracts, MMT began to experience hard times. First, the Department of Energy declined to renew a large research contract with MMT in October 1996. This news precipitated a dramatic decline in the price of MMT stock, which sent further shock waves through the investment community and the company. Second, the plan to demonstrate the process on a full commercial scale indicated serious flaws in the technology. This led to the cancellation or non-renewal of several important corporate strategic partnerships. There were occasional glimmers of hope, but still the problems persisted and then worsened. Headcount reductions and facility closings ensued until ultimately the company was forced to seek protection in U.S. Bankruptcy Court.

Learning Objectives

The two cases have been used in courses such as Sustainability in the Business Environment, Competitive Strategy, Entrepreneurship and Innovation, and Environmental Business. The learning objectives are:

1. Understand the steps necessary to get a technology-based start-up company off the ground.
2. Explore the different requirements for determining success in the laboratory and success in full-scale commercial operations.
3. To be successful, the traditional company faces the usual financial, market, and technology risks that must be overcome. In the MMT cases, the reader is introduced to political and regulatory risks—risks that can arise suddenly, with little forewarning and which can be very disruptive.

Guideline Questions

Case A

1. What was MMT's overall business model in its early phase (1989–1995) and how did it change in its later phase (1996 and beyond)?

2. What are the differences between a typical high technology start-up company and a company designed to serve the hazardous waste market?

3. What were the major financial, market, and technical risks to successful commercialization that the company faced at the end of 1995?

4. What risk avoidance and risk mitigation strategies did MMT employ?

5. Looking ahead to 1996 and beyond, what recommendations would you make to Bill Haney, the CEO? What recommendations would you make to Chris Nagel, the Chief Technology Officer?

Case B

1. What events occurred in 1996 that upset MMT's business plans? In hindsight, what could MMT have done to prevent them or mitigate their impact?

2. What lessons can be learned from this experience?

Range Resources: A Commitment to Transparency[9]

Summary

Range Resources is a publicly traded independent oil and gas company with headquarters in Pittsburgh, Pennsylvania. Since 2007, it has focused its efforts on exploring for natural gas in the Marcellus region of Ohio, West Virginia, Pennsylvania, and New York. The presence of natural gas in shale rock has been known for years but the technology to extract the gas economically is a fairly recent development. New advances in horizontal drilling and in hydraulic fracturing (called fracking) technology have dramatically changed the situation. In the fracking process, highly pressurized hydraulic fluids are injected into the well. When pumped with sufficient force, the rock formations "fracture" and create new channels for releasing and enabling the recovery of natural gas and petroleum. The rapid deployment of this technology has made the extraction of shale gas remarkably productive and important to the U.S. economy. The volume of shale gas being produced is rising so quickly that it has the potential to supply up to 50% of natural gas production in North America by 2020, reducing the country's need for imported petroleum and creating millions of new domestic jobs. However, the rapid increase in natural gas production in the United States, including in the Marcellus region, has depressed prices so that the gap between petroleum and natural gas has dramatically widened, thus further stimulating demand for natural gas. Yet because Marcellus gas is well situated in the high-energy consuming Mid-Atlantic and Northeast regions, producers of Marcellus gas have enjoyed a price premium compared with the benchmark price. For an interview with the Vice President of Geology and Exploration for Range Resources, William Zagorsky, take a look at the following video: https:// www.youtube.com/watch?v=wRKkjhtxiK4 The environmental impacts of fracking are discussed in the following video: http://www.youtube. com/watch?v=vyo9N1xkpY4

In 2004 the Environmental Protection Agency (EPA) released a study that concluded that fracking was an environmentally safe practice. Many groups criticized this report. One of the major concerns was the potential environmental and health effects of fracking on the quality of ground and surface water. Each fracking well requires about 3–4 million gallons of water to be injected into the well with chemicals added to the water to facilitate the underground fracturing process. These chemicals may include friction reducers, stabilizers, acids, and biocides. Their exact chemical composition can vary depending on the specific geologic challenges. About 50% of this contaminated water returns to the surface for treatment, where it is stored in above-ground ponds to be removed by tanker for injection into wastewater wells. The remaining "produced water" is left in the earth, where it can lead to contamination of groundwater aquifers, though the industry deems this highly unlikely.

With this background, the central issue in this case is whether Range Resources should voluntarily disclose the volume, chemical composition, and classification of their fracking fluids. A new regulatory bill has been introduced in Congress labeled the FRAC Act (Fracturing Responsibility and Awareness of Chemicals Act). If passed, the industry would be facing more stringent government regulation of the fracking process and undermine Range's ability to drive growth through the use of the hydraulic fracking process. However, the fate of this proposed legislation is uncertain and disclosure of critical information by Range might even influence the legislative process. Would the company benefit from being transparent in this regard? Should the company go against current industry practice? These are the strategic questions that are addressed in this case.

Learning Objectives

The Range Resources case can be used in courses such as Sustainability in the Business Environment, Government Business Policy, Competitive Strategy, and Environmental Business. The learning objectives are:

1. Understand the complexities of making policy and public relations decisions.
2. Explore the conflicts in decision-making processes as they relate to stakeholders at the nexus of energy and environmental issues.
3. Examine how to incorporate the benefits and risks of a controversial technology into a business strategy.

Guideline Questions

1. Why should Range Resources reveal proprietary technology and know-how to the public when it is not required?
2. How do the benefits and risks of Range Resources' short-term environmental strategy differ from its long-term environmental strategy?
3. Would you recommend that Range Resources work pro-actively with government regulators in the development of potentially costly regulations that will affect their industry?

Responding to External Consumer Pressures for Change

The cases in this section describe how some well-known brands may become the target of protester attacks. Often the company may not realize that their operations (including their extended supply chain) have left them vulnerable to these pressures. These cases are designed to build and reinforce the understanding that environmental activists and consumer protestors are stakeholders who can influence business strategy and decision making, and that there are ways for companies to develop robust business strategies in these complex situations.

McDonald's Corp.: Managing a Sustainable Supply Chain[10]

Summary

McDonald's Corporation operates a highly complex and decentralized global supply chain for its fast food restaurants. Its four largest purchases are beef, chicken, packaging, and dairy products. Although its major goals of quality, food safety, and competitive pricing have remained unchanged over the years, creating a sustainable supply chain has also received official recognition as a corporate goal. For McDonald's, this means that its global suppliers must deliver the right products at the right times for the long term, without interruption, following sustainable approaches that reduce waste, minimize risk, and provide resilience to system-wide shocks. The sustainability initiative rates suppliers on parameters such as social and economic indicators, environmental performance, and animal welfare. For McDonald's Europe, a sustainable supply chain also has to conform to regulations and customs in the European Union regarding the import of genetically modified (GM) products. European customers actively request that supplies are certified as being non-GM. However, because over 90% of global trade in soybeans is GM origin material,[11] purchasing large volumes of non-GM products over long periods of time is difficult. The main supplier of non-GM soybeans is Brazil.

In April of 2006, Greenpeace issued a report alleging that one of McDonald's primary McNuggets suppliers had fed its chickens using non-GM soybeans from recently deforested land in the Amazon. The supplier in question was Cargill, a major international producer and marketer of food and agricultural products with significant operations in Brazil. However, because Cargill was not widely known to the public and McDonald's was a highly recognized consumer brand, Greenpeace decided to focus its attack on McDonald's. The report was widely publicized and coincided with environmental activists picketing McDonald's restaurants in the EU. The report and the subsequent publicity caught McDonald's by surprise, and they needed to frame a response in a short period of time. Was the Greenpeace report accurate? Were its suppliers encouraging a deforestation program in Brazil to grow more non-GM soybeans? What influence did McDonald's have over this far-reaching supply chain?

McDonald's Europe reached out to Cargill and others in their supply chain to diagnose the problem, develop pragmatic alternatives, and find a solution. They also reached out to Greenpeace. The culmination of this effort was the development of a policy among McDonald's and its partners not to purchase soya from deforested lands and to continue to develop a more sustainable soya industry. In the wake of its successful handling of the soya issue, McDonald's formed the Sustainable Supply Chain Working Group (SSCWG) to help the company achieve its sustainable sourcing goal. The SSCWG would expand the strategy of sustainability across all aspects of McDonald's operations, as well as those of its suppliers.

In developing a supply chain that benefited a variety of stakeholders as well as the environment, McDonald's was looking to enhance its leadership role within the industry. As is often the case, the attempt to establish such a sustainable supply chain presented the company with both challenges and opportunities, such as balancing the desire for sustainability against other supply chain goals and developing a common standard across the variety of cultures where McDonald's operated. Looking forward, there were also opportunities for McDonald's to create a sustainable supply chain that effectively would become the industry standard in the minds of both consumers and suppliers.

Learning Objectives

The case has been taught in courses on Sustainability in the Business Environment, Business and the Environment, Corporate Social Responsibility, Corporate Strategy, Environmental Policy, Food Policy and Agribusiness Management, and Supply Chain Management. The learning objectives are:

1. Explore the link between corporate strategy and sustainability.
2. Understand the complexity of global supply chains from the diverse perspectives of internal and external stakeholders in a large, multinational corporation.

3. Examine how different cultural norms and practices affect corporate strategy for a global enterprise.

4. Study how NGOs, environmental activist groups, and government regulators influence corporate policy.

Guideline Questions

1. Besides sustainability, what are McDonald's major supply chain objectives, and how would you prioritize them? In what ways are these objectives mutually compatible?

2. How can a major corporation manage a global, decentralized supply chain in ways that are consistent with its sustainability initiatives?

3. How should McDonald's engage with environmental activist groups such as Greenpeace to resolve sustainability issues in its supply chain?

4. How can a global company such as McDonald's reconcile different regional perspectives about sustainability goals, protection of the environment, and economic development throughout its supply chain?

Metropolitan Water Supply Authority: Evaluating Security Risks[12]

Summary

This case describes a complex risk management challenge faced by the director of a rural metropolitan water supply facility. The facility uses chlorine gas in its water treatment, largely because chlorine is the most effective treatment available in terms of safety, cost, and environmental impact. The challenge to this decision to use chlorine came in an important security alert from the Department of Homeland Security (DHS). The DHS concern was that chlorine, a hazardous chemical, could be used by terrorists both during its transport to the treatment facility and at the facility itself. There were several alternative treatment strategies that the director considered, and each had certain advantages and disadvantages. At a high level, the choice involved centralized treatment strategies versus de-centralized treatment strategies. To simplify the analysis, the director compared the technology options by looking at the entire supply chain from raw material extraction to final consumption. He then examined each option using three environmental criteria—greenhouse gas emissions, energy consumption, and transportation system effects. He needed to weigh these factors against the homeland security risks, and make a decision.

Learning Objectives

The case can be used in courses on Sustainability in the Business Environment, Government and Business Relations, Environmental Policy, and Supply Chain Management. The learning objectives are:

1. Explore how an assessment of terrorism risks may affect corporate decision making and strategy.
2. Examine the complexities and practical considerations of managing a public enterprise in a socially responsible manner.

Guideline Questions

1. Is the DHS over-reacting to the risks chlorine poses?
2. How might a terrorist attack at the Metropolitan Water Supply Authority's facility in Unity lead to a public health emergency?
3. How would Mark argue that the risk of a terrorist attack on chlorine at the Metropolitan Water Supply Authority's facility in Unity is at an acceptable level?
4. When considering risk and potential losses, what actions could Mark take to mitigate both of the factors, to lower the probability that an event occurs, and to reduce the consequences of the event (both economic and non-economic)?

FIJI Water and Corporate Social Responsibility: Green Makeover or "Greenwashing"?[13]

Summary

The case of FIJI Water highlights how issues of environmental sustainability and corporate social responsibility (CSR) can create marketing challenges for a company as it seeks to expand into international markets.

FIJI Water was founded in 1993 to extract and bottle artesian water on the island of Viti Levu in the Fiji Islands. It was marketed as a unique, pure, and exotic product with anti-aging and immunity-boosting properties. Although the company's initial expansion into the United States in 1997 was successful and did not result in significant backlash from environmental groups, its 2004 attempt to enter the United Kingdom, a country with high quality tap water, encountered resistance. The main criticism focused on the carbon footprint associated with the water's traveling approximately 10,000 miles to market. Shortly after FIJI's entry into the market, British government officials questioned the benefit of bringing water from the other side of the Earth when essentially the same product was available out of the tap or could be brought in from much closer sources in France. Questions over the environmental impact of bottled water in general and FIJI in particular persisted and by the first quarter of 2008, owing in large part to a high profile, critical BBC documentary that focused on FIJI and a public campaign to encourage Londoners to use tap water, bottled water sales fell for the first time in years. FIJI had been singled out as an exemplar of the adverse environmental impact of the industry.

In response to its poor image, FIJI unveiled its 2008 "carbon negative" public relations campaign. The campaign had two main features. First, FIJI would calculate and disclose the carbon footprint of its products, both in terms of its own emissions and those of its partners, whom FIJI estimated to be responsible for 75% of its carbon footprint. This analysis required carbon dioxide emissions be calculated across every stage of the product lifecycle. Second, FIJI promised to offset 120% of its total carbon footprint, thus making the company carbon negative. As part of this campaign, FIJI announced in April 2008 that it had already undertaken measures to reduce its emissions. Conservationists questioned the calculation of its carbon footprint and criticized the campaign as an example of greenwashing, while continuing to extol the environmental benefits of tap water.

Learning Objectives

The case has been taught in courses on Sustainability in the Business Environment, Corporate Social Responsibility, Marketing and Innovation,

Environmental Studies, and International Business. The learning objectives are:

1. Understand the tension between CSR and a sustainable marketing strategy.
2. Provide a forum for discussing the challenges of developing creative marketing strategies in a contemporary world that values social, ethical, and environmental issues.

Guideline Questions

1. Why was the marketing strategy of FIJI Water so successful?
2. How would you determine whether FIJI Water is engaged in green-washing?
3. If you were advising FIJI Water, would you recommend that the company go carbon negative?
4. What can FIJI Water do to create a sustainable business strategy?

Mainstream Companies: Implementing Change

The cases in this section describe how traditional for-profit companies have developed creative business strategies to capture a slice of the growing sustainability market—in the retail, food, and automobile industry. Each industry sector has a host of competing technologies, environmental regulations and standards, financial considerations, and market challenges. These cases are designed to create an opportunity to evaluate these mainstream markets, to explore the challenges of implementing change in such large and diversified organizations, and to identify the benefits and risks of pursuing sustainability initiatives.

Walmart's Sustainability Strategy[14]

Summary

In October 2005 Walmart announced a major sustainability strategy to reduce its environmental impact. In addressing the issue proactively rather than defensively, as the company had done in the past, Walmart's leadership saw sustainability as an opportunity to innovate and improve its competitive position rather than as an achievement at the expense of profitability. Such a shift came in the wake of a 2004 strategic review of the legal and public relations challenges to its operations. In the course of that review, environmental impact was singled out for further analysis. Outside consultants and advisors identified three areas for improvement from both economic and sustainability perspectives—energy consumption, waste, and products. The company goal was to become more efficient in its use of energy and reduce waste while working with suppliers to improve the sustainability of its products throughout the supply chain. The three focus areas were further broken down into 14 sustainable value networks, each with its own executive sponsor. This case examines three specific value networks—seafood, electronics, and textiles.

Walmart decided that integrating sustainability into its existing operations would be a better approach than to create a separate sustainability organization because sustainability was to be an integral part of operations, not a tangential initiative carried out by a disconnected group. In implementing this new strategy, Walmart had to alter its operations and culture as well. Although the company historically had a strong inward focus, sustainability necessitated that Walmart solicit input from a variety of external organizations—consultants, NGOs, and suppliers, for example. As a result of information from its network partners, Walmart was able to adopt more ambitious goals. Developing partnerships with NGOs also enabled the company to provide its suppliers with knowledge and process improvements.

Learning Objectives

1. The case has been taught in courses on Sustainability in the Business Environment, Corporate Social Responsibility, Supply Chain Management, Environmental Entrepreneurship, and Strategy. The learning objectives are:
2. Understand how a large multinational company with no previous sensitivity to environmental or sustainability concerns opens up to external stakeholders to implement change.

3. Explore the structure of three specific value networks and the challenges required to make their global supply chains more sustainable.

4. Understand how a company can measure its environmental performance and communicate with employees, suppliers, customers, policy makers, and the public.

Guideline Questions

1. Given the perception that Walmart's customers are unwilling to pay a premium for environmentally friendly products, how can the company justify its sustainability strategy?

2. Which of the three value networks—electronics, seafood and textiles—has been the most successful in creating a more sustainable supply chain?

3. Besides offering to pay a supplier more, what policies can Walmart employ to motivate its suppliers to reduce their environmental footprints? How can Walmart encourage the adoption of game-changer technologies or practices among its suppliers?

Frito-Lay North America: The Making of a Net Zero Snack Chip[15]

Summary

Frito-Lay, a division of Pepsi Cola, is the largest manufacturer of snack foods in the United States. The case of Frito-Lay's net zero snack chip highlights how one company used sustainability as a means of driving innovation that improved performance by reducing its environmental impact and its costs, while achieving an improved market position. A "net zero snack" means that the total greenhouse gas emissions to manufacture the snack are zero.

Although Frito-Lay experienced healthy growth into the 1990s, there was concern over increasing cost and price volatility of energy resources and the availability of water resources in the future. Going beyond their traditional regulatory role, Frito-Lay's environmental compliance group took the lead to focus on resource conservation as a strategy for reducing costs. The initial results of this effort were positive, and in 1999 they expanded to a company-wide initiative to reduce resource usage and costs. The next 8 years brought the design, building, and implementation of a variety of projects. By 2007, against sales of more than $1.5 billion, Frito-Lay's conservation efforts were saving the company $55 million per year in reduced expenses. Beyond the direct savings, the initiative also provided the company with valuable data about operations, productivity, and resource usage.

Building on the success of their conservation effort, Frito-Lay next looked to reduce not only its emissions per unit of production, but its absolute emissions. Growth would be more than offset by increased efficiency and conservation efforts. This goal resulted in the 2008 proposal to convert an existing plant into a net-zero one that would maximize renewable energy and water conservation. Working with the National Renewable Energy Laboratory, Frito-Lay chose its facility in Casa Grande, AZ for this pilot program. To meet its goals, the plant used solar energy to reduce energy-related greenhouse gas emissions and a nanofiltration system to process wastewater into drinking water throughout the production process. Such process changes were projected to reduce consumption of water by 75%, natural gas by 80%, and purchased electricity by 90%. For a brief overview of the net zero project, take a look at the following video: http://www.youtube.com/watch?v=0U5_pKoWc1s

Learning Objectives

The case has been taught in courses on Sustainability in the Business Environment, Operations Strategy, Environmental Entrepreneurship and Environmental Management. The learning objectives are:

1. Understand how a large well-known company responds to changing conditions with respect to the environment and energy price volatility.
2. Discuss the decision-making process within the company that resulted in the net-zero facility.
3. Understand the relationships among sustainability innovation strategies and the supply chain.

Guideline Questions

1. If you are the company's resource conservation team leader, what are the most important factors in considering the net-zero facility decision?

2. Considering the financial, market, and technical risks and benefits of the project, what are the arguments for/against the investment to create a net-zero plant? Prepare to argue your case in front of the company's senior management team.

3. What is the importance of leadership to sustainability innovation?

Launch of the Ford Fiesta Diesel: The World's Most Efficient Car[16]

Summary

The Ford Motor Company is an icon of the automobile industry. Founded by Henry Ford in 1903, it was an early innovator of novel manufacturing methods offering fuel efficient models across a broad product line. Ford led in market share in the industry until the late 1920s, when its sales were surpassed by General Motors. Ford, like other U.S. automobile makers, was hit hard by the oil crises of 1973 and 1979 that saw gasoline prices spike upward and sales plummet. To deal with the energy crisis, the U.S. government imposed fuel economy standards on the automobile industry. Ford resisted the government regulations and converted its production to more fuel efficient models only as necessary to comply with the law. Japanese competitors, on the other hand, seized the opportunity and entered the North American market with small, inexpensive, fuel-efficient cars that quickly gained a 20% market share. Domestic auto manufacturers fell on hard times for the next decade as consumers perceived the domestic product as a shoddy alternative to imported models.

Ford spent the next 20 years developing new fuel-efficient technologies. In 2000, it created a concept car capable of 72 miles per gallon (mpg); and in 2008, it unveiled a new sports utility vehicle capable of 120 mpg. Yet each time Ford engineers developed new fuel efficient technologies, they were overruled by business and marketing executives who concluded that the fuel-efficient cars would not be popular with the car-buying public, or that the cost of re-tooling factories was prohibitive. As late as 2004, Ford ranked at the bottom of the industry in fuel efficiency, according to the U.S. Environmental Protection Agency.

The case describes the situation in November 2008 when Ford announced the launch of the highly anticipated Fiesta Diesel to the European market. At 65 mpg, the Fiesta was one of the most fuel-efficient cars in the world, easily beating Toyota's Prius hybrid, rated at 51 mpg. European consumers embraced the car and it quickly gained market acceptance. However, Ford executives decided to keep the technology out of the United States for the foreseeable future. Factored into this decision was the current low market share for diesel engines in the United States, the perception that diesel engines were dirty, smoky, smelly, and slow, the high cost of manufacturing in the United States, and the high break-even sales requirements. Could Ford create a different market entry strategy? Should it launch the model in another region of the world or continue selling it exclusively in Europe?

Learning Objectives

The case has been taught in courses on Sustainability in the Business Environment, Operations Strategy, International Business Strategy, and Energy and the Environment. The learning objectives are:

1. Understand the decision-making process within Ford that resulted in limiting the diesel technology to the European market.
2. Explore the use of focus group information, which may be incorrect and out-of-date, to influence the introduction of new technology.
3. Examine how a large, well-known company responds to changing environment and energy price conditions.

Guideline Questions

1. Do you support Ford's decision to forego the introduction of the Fiesta diesel engine in the United States? Why or why not?
2. How can Ford leverage its technological strength in clean diesel engines to serve the North American market?

Sustainability and Corporate Finance

In the previous sections of this chapter, we summarize business case studies in categories that highlight specific aspects of a company's business model or circumstances that a business may encounter. For example, we follow the progression of Burt's Bees from an entrepreneurial and quirky business to an extremely successful and profitable business for its founders, employees, and investors, while maintaining its "greater good" vision. In the Herman Miller, Clorox, and Whole Foods cases, we examine different strategic approaches to tap the "green" consumer market while earning significant financial returns in the process. In the Du Pont Freon Products case, we explore a complex situation in which scientific and regulatory pressures required a large multinational corporation to do a complete "about face" with its entire product line, phasing out the incumbent products while introducing a new slate of more environmentally friendly products. In the process, Du Pont was able to navigate the transition successfully while improving its strategic position in the industry and reap significant financial rewards, as well. In the Walmart case, we investigated how the world's largest retailer tackled the daunting challenge of making their global supply chain more sustainable while improving their bottom line. Lastly, in the Frito-Lay case, we studied the strategic and financial decision to adopt energy-saving and water conservation technologies that will allow its Arizona factory to drastically reduce their carbon dioxide emissions.

Thus, the business case for sustainability is illustrated in a variety of ways throughout the previous sections—by creating a sustainable business model from inception, by tapping new revenue streams from "green" customers, by effectively responding to external regulatory pressure, and by revamping existing supply chains that are not sustainable for the long term.

In the remainder of this section, we describe additional cases at the intersection of sustainability and corporate finance. These cases are designed to help build understanding of the market barriers to these ventures and their technical, market, and financial risks.

Patagonia[17]

Summary

Patagonia is an iconic name in the outdoor apparel and equipment industry. The company was founded in the 1970s by entrepreneur Yvon

Chouinard, an avid mountain climber, skier, and surfer. The company's basic business philosophy combines two key elements: a commitment to produce high quality products that are also environmentally friendly. The company's commitment to quality was supported by its significant investment in research and development, which resulted in numerous innovative new products and materials, such as Synchilla®, a soft, non-pilling double-faced fleece fabric. The company's commitment to the environment was evident when it switched its entire line of sportswear to organically grown cotton in 1996. Patagonia's commitment to sustainability extends to its supply chain and logistics partners, and to its recent Product Lifecycle Initiative to "reduce, repair, reuse, and recycle."

Under Chouinard's leadership, the company achieved significant financial success. Sales grew by 6% per year for most of the 2000s and reached $330 million in 2010. Gross margins in 2010 were 52%, while operating margins amounted to 8.1%. The company was spending less than 1% of sales on marketing, far less than the industry norm. Patagonia created value through high quality and innovative products, environmental commitment, and ironclad guarantee to take back unsatisfactory products from customers. It charged about 20% more than the competition.

For a short background on Yvon Chouinard, the company's business mission and strategy, and its environmental initiatives, see this short Internet video: https://www.youtube.com/watch?v=O3TwU-Lu-Wjw

Learning Objectives

The case has been taught in courses on Sustainability in the Business Environment, Business Strategy, and Entrepreneurship. The learning objectives are:

1. Explore a business model that seeks to build environmental and sustainability objectives into its core business strategy.
2. Understand the link between the value creation/value capture model of Patagonia and company valuation.

Guideline Questions

1. Why has Patagonia been so successful to date?
2. If Mr. Chouinard decides to sell the company, how would you prepare estimates of the firm's value?

Next Era's EarthEra Renewable Energy Trust[18]

Summary

NextEra is the largest generator of wind and solar power in North America, reporting a net income of over $1 billion in 2011. NextEra operates more than 100 facilities in 17 states and 4 Canadian provinces. Approximately 95% of their electricity generation comes from clean or renewable sources. This case describes NextEra's launch of a new initiative to increase investment in renewable energy.

To encourage greater investment and use of renewable energy, twenty nine states have instituted Renewable Portfolio Standards (RPS). These regulations place an obligation on the electricity supply companies in that state to produce a specified fraction of their electricity from renewable energy sources such as wind, solar, biomass, and geothermal. California, for example, has specified that 33% of its electricity be generated from renewable sources by 2020; the mandate for Kansas is 20% by 2020. Companies that generate electricity earn certificates for every unit of electricity they produce and can sell these along with their electricity to supply companies. Supply companies then pass the certificates, called Renewable Energy Certificates (RECs) to the appropriate regulatory body to demonstrate their compliance with the RPS. By definition, an REC entitles its owner to the environmental attributes (but not the actual electrical power) from the generation of 1 megawatt-hour of renewably generated electricity. Because it is a market mandate, the RECs trade freely like any commodity and are subject to market volatility. Growth for RECs was strong in the early to mid-2000s when conventional energy prices were high, the regulatory climate was favorable, government tax credits and subsidies were available, and financing costs were low. After the 2008 financial crisis, however, the economic, political, and financial conditions changed, and investment in renewable energy projects waned.

In 2009, NextEra decided to launch a new REC purchase program that would allow customers to reduce their carbon footprint and accelerate the investment in renewable energy projects. Called EarthEra Renewable Energy Trust, this new program's business model had four main elements—companies or individuals could purchase a REC from NextEra; EarthEra Trust received all proceeds from the transaction; NextEra could use the funds to build new renewable projects; and EarthEra could operate the new facility to generate more renewable energy. Given the economic realities of a sluggish economy, diminished interest in environmental programs, and rising consumer skepticism along with corporate greenwashing, the marketing team of NextEra needed a creative strategy to be successful.

Learning Objectives

The case has been taught in courses on Sustainability in the Business Environment, Entrepreneurial Finance, Energy and the Environment, Environmental Management. The learning objectives are:

1. Understand the structure and characteristics of the REC market.
2. Categorize the priority market segments for EarthEra RECs, and the most likely prospective firms within this segment.
3. Explore whether NextEra would reap greater benefits from a broad marketing effort or a narrow one.

Guideline Questions

1. If you were advising NextEra, what industry market segment would you suggest offers the greatest potential reward? Why?
2. What are the characteristics of the firm within the target market segment that offers the greatest potential acceptance rate?

The Dual Sustainability of Wind Energy[19]

Summary

Entrepreneurs and innovators continue searching for cost-effective sources of alternative energy, especially from renewable sources like wind and solar. This case study looks at what conditions are necessary for a large wind farm consisting of 100 turbines to achieve two metrics for sustainability—environmental performance and financial profitability. A variety of federal and state government programs provide financial incentives to encourage private investment in wind energy projects such as accelerated depreciation, production tax credits, and renewable energy credits. In addition, technology advances in wind energy have reduced costs dramatically over the past several years.

This case presents data for the wind farm project suitable for financial analysis and sensitivity testing from cost, technology, public policy, and investment perspectives.

Learning Objectives

The case has been taught in courses on Sustainability in the Business Environment, Entrepreneurial Finance, and Energy and the Environment. The learning objectives are:

1. Understand the structure and characteristics of the wind energy market.
2. Identify how government policy tools have been utilized to encourage wind energy.
3. Apply standard financial tools like net present value and sensitivity analysis to understand the financial viability and risk of wind energy projects.

Guideline Questions

1. When is government intervention in energy markets desirable?
2. What are the key economic drivers for this wind energy project?
3. Given the assumptions in the case, would you recommend investing in this project? Why or why not?
4. If government financial incentives like the production tax credit expire, would your recommendation change?

Summary

Sustainability is garnering greater public attention and debate, and nowhere is this more evident that in the corporate sector. Most publicly-traded corporations publish sustainability or CSR reports on their Internet sites. Some companies clearly build sustainability into their strategy and use it gain competitive advantage. Others are cautiously adopting more sustainable business practices, while still others make environmental claims that are difficult to substantiate. This latter group of companies, the "greenwashers," uses deceptive advertisement to promote the perception of environmentally friendly policies.

Given the highly complex nature of sustainability in business today, the case study approach is a useful pedagogical tool to explore the decision-making framework in a variety of companies and a variety of contexts. The companies we've looked at in these case studies range in size from small entrepreneurial ventures to major international organizations. The business case studies we've summarized are from a variety of disciplines—strategy, general management, operations, entrepreneurship, marketing, supply chain, and finance. Since we believe that the corporate sector will play a key role in solving the long-term issues related to sustainability, there is much that we can learn by examining this collection of case studies. They help us to appreciate the complexity of decision-making and the new way of thinking, the systems approach, that best supports sustainability. We highlight below some the key lessons from this collection of business case studies:

- **General management:** Business strategy is never based on the profit motive alone in organizations committed to sustainability. Mission-oriented businesses that strive to meet the triple bottom line imperative can thrive in high growth industries against traditional competitors, as witnessed by the case studies on Burt's Bees, Whole Foods, and Patagonia.

- **Operations:** Eliminating waste and inefficiencies in operations and minimizing environmental risks will not only improve profitability, it can enhance environmental performance and societal well-being. In addition, redesigning a product using concepts like C2C requires collaboration between many different groups in a company (operations, marketing, procurement, R&D, etc). We examined how companies are tackling these issues in the case studies on Herman Miller, Frito-Lay, Du Pont, and Walmart.

- **Entrepreneurship:** New creative approaches to doing business, particularly when they address market failures, can be profitable, good for the environment, and provide societal benefits for large numbers of people. Not every entrepreneurial venture is a success, and we often learn more from an analysis of failed ventures that from successful ones. We provide examples of successful ventures like Burt's Bees and the three social entrepreneurs in contrast to the meteoric rise and then the collapse of MMT.

- **Marketing:** Imaginative approaches to the creation and capture of value requires an effective marketing effort built on actual sustainability rather than greenwashing. We examined how some companies approach the task of building consumer trust, like Clorox, Patagonia, and Herman Miller, while other companies used more questionable practices like FIJI Water.

- **Supply chain:** Supply chain managers recognize the enormous opportunities that globalization, outsourcing, and increased stakeholder expectations represent as a business enterprise strives to become more sustainable. To capitalize on these opportunities requires senior management commitment, financial and human resources, and creativity. We examined how companies approach these issues from different perspectives and circumstances, and we saw some of the major challenges of implementation. The examples include McDonald's, Walmart, Ford, and FIJI Water.

- **Finance:** Financial managers are an important part of the triple bottom line assessment, and financial analysis plays a role in nearly every business decision that involves sustainability—project finance (Frito-Lay), business process improvement (Herman Miller), firm valuation (Patagonia), pricing (Clorox and Whole Foods), risk management (Ford), procurement and the supply chain (Walmart and McDonald's), and corporate governance (Range Resources).

Going Forward to Chapter 5

The examples in this chapter illustrate the business case for sustainability in every functional area of a business enterprise: in entrepreneurial ventures that are built on sustainability principles, in tapping new revenue streams from "green" customers, in effectively responding to external regulatory pressure, and in revamping existing supply chains that are not sustainable for the long term. Now that we have reviewed cases that speak to sustainability challenges within the business context, we move forward to the final task, which is summarizing our message on an introduction to sustainability in the business context.

CHAPTER 5

Concluding Thoughts

Learning Objectives

- Synthesize the concepts of sustainability
- Commit to a call to action

The concept of sustainability in the business press emerged about twenty years ago. Since that time, the concept has evolved from a vague goal to "save the planet" to become a strategic imperative accompanied by improved internal business processes, assessment and measurement tools, and tactics to enhance performance. Corporate leaders can no longer claim, as Milton Friedman supposedly declared, that "the business of business is business." Rather, the public now expects and demands corporations to be responsible and embrace financial integrity and transparency (as regulated by Sarbanes-Oxley and, Dodd-Frank), worker health and safety (as regulated by the Occupational Safety and Health Administration), product safety (as regulated by the Consumer Product Safety Commission), and protection of the environment (as regulated by the Environmental Protection Administration). We live in an age of increasing corporate accountability. If a business expects to survive for the long haul, it must adhere to ever higher standards of behavior and continuously develop more sustainable ways of doing business. In this chapter we summarize the major lessons learned in the previous chapters and provide our concluding thoughts about the future of sustainability.

- **Business needs to reformulate products and markets.**
  Using the systems and tools of sustainability, we examined how businesses can reformulate products using the principles of cradle-to-cradle design, reducing waste during manufacture, streamlining the supply chain, and reusing or recycling material at the end of a product's life to minimize or eliminate

the amount of material that must be deposited in landfills. We also explored the assessment and measurement tools for sustainability, including the Global Reporting Initiative, Carbon Disclosure Project, carbon footprinting and water footprinting. These are important tools to assess the current situation for a company.

These systems and tools for sustainability are similar to those a physician uses taking blood pressure and cholesterol readings for a middle-aged, fairly overweight patient. The tests provide meaningful data to the doctor who, after consulting with the patient's history, advises the patient that if current trends continue, the patient will likely suffer adverse health outcomes such as a stroke or heart attack. The patient may ask, "What can I do to reverse or slow down this prognosis?" The doctor responds, "Adjust your diet, cut out sweets, and go to the gym three days a week for at least 30 minutes." The patient, unfortunately, decides, "I really enjoy food, especially sweets, and I really hate going to the gym. Don't you have a pill that will allow me to eat everything in sight and still lose weight?" For this patient, the diagnosis is correct but the inability to implement the behavior modifications means that the patient will not be able to reverse the negative health consequences.

Many businesses find themselves in a parallel predicament. The assessment and diagnosis can be done with precision, but the devil lies in the details of the follow-up implementation. The re-design of one product line based on the cradle-to-cradle protocol is exceeding difficult; for a company to re-design all its product lines is a monumental task. Analyzing the company's supply chain is another labor intensive and complex task that can be done with accuracy, often accompanied with carefully constructed measures of carbon dioxide emissions and water usage. The task of developing and implementing strategies to revise the supply chain while reducing greenhouse gas emissions and water usage, however, requires commitment, capital, worker training, and often a long phase-in period.

Despite these challenges, there is no more powerful institution in the world to enable the planet to become more sustainable than the business community. Yet businesses often feel trapped because they define value creation from a narrow perspective, they utilize outmoded product supply chains that were created decades ago, and they are tethered to a short-term financial mindset. In our opinion, business needs a broader view. Andrew Savitz calls this "the sustainability sweet spot: the place where the pursuit of profit blends seamlessly with the pursuit of the common good."[1] Society's needs are enormous—improved health care, shelter, assistance for an aging population, nutritious food, financial security, less environmental damage, and clean air and ample water. The business community has the skills, experience, and resources to meet these societal needs. Businesses can design innovative products and services to meet these needs; they can create eco-efficient supply chains to deliver products to customers; and they have the marketing skills to motivate customers to incorporate these products into their life style in a sustainable manner. We explored these issues in the previous chapters and examined examples of the sweet spot in our business case studies in Chapter 4. We remain optimistic that as long as customers vote with their wallets and demand more sustain-able products, business will create goods and services that meet these needs.

- **Business needs to focus on more than profit.** The narrow, profit-centered view of business is no longer acceptable to the general public. The new view is summed up by the phrase, the triple bottom line, in which companies are expected to bal-ance the need for profit with a desire to safeguard the planet and with a concern for people—employees, the community, customers, and other stakeholders.

Michael Porter, Professor at Harvard University, calls this new paradigm, "creating shared value."[2] Corporations commonly state their purpose as one that seeks to maximize *shareholder value*, an objective that puts the equity owners of a corporation above all other interests. In Porter's view, "the concept of shared value can be defined as policies and operating practices that enhance the competitiveness of a company while simultaneously advancing the economic and social conditions in the communities in which it operates. Shared value creation focuses on identifying and expanding the connections between societal and economic progress."[3]

This concept of shared value is quite different from corporate social responsibility or corporate philanthropy. The latter are discretionary activities quite apart from the core value creation activities of the company. They serve as a good public relations message to the community. As we learned from the material in the previous chapters, firms that are guided by the shared value vision develop strategies and practices that create economic value by creating social value. These firms are the wave of the future.

- **Government regulation needs to be a positive force for change.** If done properly, government regulation can encourage innovation, protect people, stimulate economic growth, facilitate fair competition, and improve the functioning of markets. Unfortunately, government regulation sometimes acts in the opposite manner. Government regulation, if done poorly, can discourage innovation, protect jobs (not people), limit economic growth, impede competition, and hamper the normal functioning of the market. In markets for natural resources like water and petroleum, poorly designed government regulations can promote over-consumption by failing to set prices that reflect true costs. These poorly designed regulations can also impose burdensome reporting requirements and unnecessary administrative costs.

  A few guidelines for good government regulatory practices include setting clear goals and objectives, setting prices that reflect true costs, setting performance standards and phase-in schedules without imposing the means to achieve the standards, and establishing measurement systems that allow for proper reporting of results. It is also important to create a dynamic rule-making process that can accommodate changes over time as companies develop new innovative products and services and market conditions evolve.

An example of a government directive that serves as a positive force for change is extended producer responsibility regulation, or take-back laws. First enacted in several European countries in the 1990s, 25 states in the United States have now adopted these regulations for specific classes of products such as electronic devices. The concept is consistent with the principles of sustainability—make the manufacturer of a product responsible for the entire life cycle of the product, which in certain instances includes taking the product back for disassembly, recycling, and ultimate disposal. In addition, the cost of recycling and disposal is borne by the manufacturer, not by the local municipal government or other waste collection service. This form of regulation accomplishes several desirable societal goals: Manufacturers are incentivized to design more sustainable products that are easily taken apart; the products contain less toxic material; and product prices will better reflect full costs across the entire product life cycle. Ideal products are those which follow the cradle-to-cradle protocol.

As we discovered in the readings and several case studies, government policies can have dramatic and powerful effects on company performance—both positive and negative. Companies that can understand how to shape effective policies will be well positioned to benefit from them while, at the same time, benefiting society.

A Call to Action

We have now taken you, the reader, on a journey that presented you with an opportunity to increase your awareness of the sustainability practices in the world around you and have given you an introduction to the systems and tools to guide you on this journey. Awareness alone, however, is only the first step in creating a more sustainable world. As the Chinese philosopher Lao Tzu observed in the sixth century B.C., "The journey of a thousand miles begins with one step." You need to begin your own journey now and take steps to close the gap between awareness and action. It will not be an easy or a straightforward task, and it needs your attention on multiple levels.

- First, as an *individual*, you need to become an educated, environmentally-aware consumer. This means that you make life-style decisions that respect the principles of sustainability—namely, meeting your needs today without compromising the ability of future generations to meet their needs.
- Second, as a *member of a community*, you need to encourage collective action. It has never been easier to reach out to your friends, neighbors, business associates, and the public at large to catalyze collective action. According to the International Telecommunication Union in Geneva, Switzerland, there are nearly as many cell phone subscriptions as inhabitants in the world.[4] In some regions of the world, more people have cell phones than access to clean drinking water or proper sanitation. Social media sites like Facebook, Twitter, and Qzone (China's largest active social network website) make it relatively easy to reach millions of people instantly. There are more than 1 billion Facebook registered uses, 500 million Twitter uses, and nearly 600 million Qzone users.
- Third, as an *employee* (current, past, or prospective), you can make your voice heard in identifying, analyzing, and implementing improvements in business processes to better protect the planet while meeting the other needs of the business.
- Fourth, as a *citizen* in your local community, you need to be an active participant in the political process so that government officials can better educate the public about the principles of sustainability and make wise political choices. Government must play a positive role in creating a more sustainable world, and you, as a citizen and voter, can support sustainable government initiatives and legislation.

In this book, we have focused on the positive opportunities of sustainability in the business world as opposed to the negative challenges of overcoming lethargy, indifference, and the perspective that sustainability is someone else's problem or that the government will take care of this issue. Moving forward, we need to recognize that we live in an interdependent and interconnected world. The lines between individuals, business, government, and non-governmental organizations are blurred. We each are members of all these institutions in one fashion or another: By purchasing sustainable goods and services, we are voting with our wallets; by working for companies or organizations that have adopted sustainable practices, we are voting with the sweat of our brow; by electing thoughtful and intelligent public officials, we are voting through the ballot box; and with our philanthropy, we are voting with our charitable donations to NGOs.

Sustainability in the business environment is here to stay because it makes economic and business sense. Even though the trade-offs are complex, even though there are ambiguity and conflicting perspectives, the business community needs to embrace the principles of sustainability. Businesses, at all levels and in all functional areas, can lead the way because they have the skills, resources, and management capability to achieve what society needs and what even the best-intentioned government programs can rarely match. In short, we have no alternative—we are all in this together. We are all stakeholders in building sustainable businesses.

Notes

Chapter 1

1. Costanza et al. (1997).
2. Huesemann and Huesemann (2011).
3. United Nations Environmental Programme (1992).
4. Friends of the Earth (2005).
5. Brundtland (1987).
6. Plambeck and Denend (2007).
7. A value chain is different from a supply chain. A value chain is the set of inter-related activities that a firm performs in order to create value for its product or service. For example, an expert diamond cutter can create value by transforming an unfinished diamond into a fine gemstone.
8. Laszlo, Christensen, Fogel, Wagner, and Whitehouse (2010).
9. Lane, Maznevski, and Mendenhall (2004).
10. Paraphrasing the U.N.'s World Commission on Environment and Development, Our Common Future Report; see Brundtland (1987).

Chapter 2

1. Not all greenhouse gases have the same global warming potential. Besides carbon dioxide, gases like methane, nitrous oxide, sulfur hexafluoride, and chlorofluoro-carbons also contribute to global warming. To adjust for these differences, which can be quite large, scientists have established a method for converting emissions to a common unit using carbon dioxide as a basis.
2. DALY is a World Health Organization standard. DALY is a measure of overall disease burden expressed as the number of years lost due to ill-health, disability, or early death.
3. This measure assumes that a year of life lived in perfect health is worth 1 QALY and that a year of life lived in a state of less than this perfect health is worth less than 1.
4. This comparison has created a series of competing studies with differing con-clusions. For a summary, readers are referred to this ABC News story: http://abcnews.go.com/Technology/story?id=789465&page=1#.Ubjp-ZxQBmB
5. Plambeck and Denend (2007), p. 18.
6. Plambeck and Denend (2007), p. 21.
7. On December 8, 2006, the Greater London Authority (GLA) became the first public-sector body to publish a sustainable procurement policy, promising to award a "distinct competitive advantage" to those companies that demonstrated

a commitment to sustainable procurement concerns. The GLA group has defined "responsible procurement" as the purchase of goods, works, and services in a socially and environmentally responsible way that delivers value for money and benefits to the contracting authority and to London. See http://www. london.gov.uk/media/press_releases_mayoral/londons-regional-government-sets-benchmark-fair-procurement

8. World Bank (2007), p. 14.
9. In 2006, Rob van Hattum explored this concept through interviews with leading proponents in a documentary film of the same name. See http://icarusfilms. com/new2007/waste.html
10. Ditz and Ranganathan (1997), p. 4.
11. Ditz and Ranganathan (1997), p. 5, citing Wackernagel and Rees (1996).
12. Kolk (1999).
13. U.S. Geological Survey (n.d.).
14. See unglobalcompact.org/AboutTheGC/TheTenPrinciples/index.html
15. United Nations Global Compact (n.d.).
16. Confino (2012).
17. Confino (2012).
18. Global Reporting Initiative (n.d.).
19. See www.cdproject.net
20. Newell (2010).
21. CDC, Leadership Indexes and the CDP 2012 disclosure and performance scores, at https://www.cdproject.net/en-us/results/pages/leadership-index. aspx (accessed July 27, 2013).
22. Wright, Kemp, and Williams (2011), pp. 61–72.
23. Water Footprint Network (n.d.).
24. See http://hdr.undp.org/en/humandev
25. http://www.undp.org
26. Pinkham (n.d.).
27. Taylor (2006).
28. Bonini and Gorner (2011).
29. White (2009).

Chapter 3

1. Lemonich (2009).
2. Mitchell (1998), p. 41.
3. As referenced in Mitchell (1998), p. 51, from Habermas (1985), The Theory of Communicative Action.
4. Thomas, Lane, and Maznevski (2008). This section draws the connection between re-vision and reflective thinking from this work.
5. After the figure developed in Thomas et al. (2008).

6. Gro Harlem Brundtland was chair of the United Nations World Commission on Environment and Development, commonly referred to as the Brundtland Commission, in 1987, whose report, Our Common Future, established sustainability as a development model.
7. World Population Prospects (2011).
8. Sharon Bloyd-Peshkin has addressed these issues in her 2009 feature in In These Times and uses the terms functional obsolescence and fashion obsolescence for these design approaches.
9. Begley (2010).
10. Ecological Society of America (2000).
11. Millennium Ecosystem Assessment (2005).
12. Costanza et al. (1997).
13. Costanza et al. (1997).
14. Polasky (2008), pp. 42–46.
15. Parington (1928).
16. Molina and Zaelke (2012).
17. Bracmort and Lattanzio (2013).
18. Prinn (2009).
19. Crutzen (2006).
20. Morgan (2009).
21. For the cost of iron fertilization see Worstall (2012). For the cost of a ton of carbon dioxide see Environmental and Energy Study Institute (2012).
22. Trick et al. (2010).
23. Cao and Caldeira (2010).
24. Tilmes, Müller, and Salawitch (2008).
25. Robock, Oman, and Stenchikov (2008).
26. 2030 Water Resources Group (2009).
27. U.S. Government Accountability Office (2002), p. 10.
28. The Johnson Foundation (2012), p. 2.
29. The Johnson Foundation (2012), p. 11.
30. Hall and Lobina (2009), p. 1.
31. Hall and Lobina (2009), p. 2.
32. This section is based on the report by Sher (2012).
33. Kuuskraa, Stevens, Leeuwen, and Moodhe (2011), p. 4.
34. Brent crude oil price in dollars per barrel and Henry Hub natural gas price in dollars per million Btu.
35. See http://www.eia.gov/todayinenergy/detail.cfm?id=5830
36. PriceWaterhouseCoopers (2011), p. 1.
37. IHS CERA (2012), p. 2.
38. IHS CERA (2012), p. 8.
39. Yergin (2012).
40. Schramm (2011).

41. Testimony of Katy Dunlap before the Subcommittee on Water and Power of the Committee on Energy and Natural Resources, October 20, 2011.

42. For example, see the background paper prepared for the National Climate Assessment by Robert Howarth and others, "Methane Emissions from Natural Gas Systems," February 25, 2012.

43. National Research Council (2012), p. 3.

44. For further information, see http://www.sehn.org/wing.html

45. Commission of the European Communities (2001), p. 5.

46. Church and Regis (2012), p. 11.

47. Graham (2004), p. 2.

48. Tversky and Kahneman (1974), pp. 1124–1131.

Chapter 4

1. Winig and Walthieu (2007).

2. Phills and Denend (2005).

3. Lee and Bony (2007).

4. Cammarata, Gough, Moss, Nowygord, and Springer (2010).

5. Wells and Haglock (2008).

6. Vietor and Reinhardt (1995).

7. Hoffman (2010a).

8. Hoffman (2010b).

9. Avrahami et al. (2011).

10. Goldberg and Yagan (2007).

11. This section is based on The Global GM Market: Implications for the European Food Chain by Brookes, Craddock, and Kniel (2005).

12. McNett and Whitfield (2013).

13. McMaster and Nowak (2009).

14. Plambeck and Denend (2007).

15. Larson and Teichman (2009).

16. Spital and Wesley (2010).

17. Reinhardt, Casadesus-Masanell, and Kim (2010)

18. Agins et al. (2012).

19. Welch and Venkateswaran (2009).

Chapter 5

1. Savitz (2006), p. 22.

2. Porter and Kramer (2011).

3. Porter and Kramer (2011), p. 66.

4. International Telecommunications Union (2013).

References

2030 Water Resources Group. (2009). *Charting our water future: Economic frameworks to inform decision-making.* Retrieved March 9, 2013, from: http://www.2030waterresourcesgroup.com/water_full/Charting_Our_Water_Future_Final.pdf

Agins, J., Bhatia, R., Cunningham, A., George, N., Gonzalez-Kriesberg, D., & Mattson, J. (2012). *NextEra's EarthEra renewable energy trust: Marketing America's renewable energy future* (Case 1-429-232). Ann Arbor, MI: Global Lens.

Avrahami, T., Barclay, P., Barjum, S., Berent, L., Braun, A., & Calderon, L. (2011). *Range Resources: A commitment to transparency* (Case 1-429-168). Ann Arbor, MI: Global Lens.

Begley, S. (2010). *Green and clueless.* Retrieved March 3, 2013, from *Newsweek*: http://www.thedailybeast.com/newsweek/2010/08/17/why-we-re-so-clueless-about-being-green.html (Reprinted in *Taking sides*, pp. 12–13, by R. W. Taylor, 2012, New York, NY: McGraw-Hill)

Bloyd-Peshkin, S. (2009). *Built to trash: Is 'heirloom design' the cure for consumption?* Retrieved March 3, 2013, from In These Times: http://inthesetimes.com/article/5023/built_to_trash (Reprinted in *Taking sides*, pp. 6–11, by R. W. Taylor, 2012, New York, NY: McGraw-Hill)

Bonini, S. & Gorner, S. (2011, October). *The business of sustainability: McKinsey Global Survey Results.* Retrieved December 10, 2012, from McKinsey & Company, Insights & Publications: www.mckinseyquarterly.com/Energy_Resources_Materials/Environment/The_business_of_sustainability_McKinsey_Global_Survey_results_2867

Bracmort, K. & Lattanzio, R. K. (2013). *Geoengineering: Governance and technology policy.* Washington, DC: Congressional Research Service.

Brookes, G., Craddock, N., & Kniel, B. (2005, September). *The global GM market: Implications for the European food chain.* Retrieved February 18, 2013, from: http://www.salmone.org/wp-content/uploads/2007/09/brookes-report-lr.pdf

Brundtland, G. H. (1987). Our common future: Report of the World Commission on Environment and Development. United Nations World Commission on Environment and Development. Retrieved February 4, 2013, from: http://www.un-documents.net/wced-ocf.htm

Cammarata, C., Gough, J., Moss, B., Nowygord, A., & Springer, N. (2010). *Clorox goes green* (Case 1-429-087). Ann Arbor, MI: Global Lens.

Cao, L., & Caldeira, K. (2010). Can ocean iron fertilization mitigate ocean acidification? *Climatic Change 99*(1–2), 303–311.

Church, G., & Regis, E. (2012). *Regenesis: How synthetic biology will reinvent nature and ourselves.* New York, NY: Basic Books.

Commission of the European Communities. (2001). *White paper: Strategy for a future chemicals policy.* Retrieved on March 3, 2013 from http://eur-lex.europa.eu/LexUriServ/site/en/com/2001/com2001_0088en01.pdf

Confino, J. (2012, March 26). *Cleaning up the Global Compact: Dealing with corporate free riders.* Retrieved January 13, 2013, from *The Guardian*: http://www.guardian.co.uk/sustainable-business/cleaning-up-un-global-compact-green-wash

Costanza, R., d'Arge, R., de Groot, R., Farber, S., Grasso, M., Hannon, B., Limburg, K., Naeem, S., O'Neill, R. V., Paruelo, J., Raskin, R. G., Sutton, P., & Belt. M. V. (1997). The value of the world's ecosystem services and natural capital. *Nature 387*(6630), 253–261.

Crutzen, P. J. (2006). Albedo enhancement by stratospheric sulfur injections: A contribution to resolve a policy dilemma? *Climatic Change 77*(3–4), 211–219.

Ditz, D., & Ranganathan, J. (1997). *Measuring up: Toward a common platform for measuring corporate financial performance.* Washington, DC: World Resources Institute.

Dunlap, K. (2011). *Shale gas production and water resources in the eastern United States.* Retrieved March 2, 2013: http://www.energy.senate.gov/public/index.cfm/files/serve?File_id=1cbe5c49-aa41-4bec-a6b7-992068c59666

Ecological Society of America. (2000). Retrieved February 14, 2013, from: http://www.esa.org/ecoservices/comm/body.comm.fact.ecos.html

Elkington, J. (1999). *Cannibals with forks: The triple bottom line of 21st century business.* Hoboken, NJ: Wiley.

Environmental and Energy Study Institute. (2012, October). *Fact sheet: Carbon pricing around the world.* Retrieved from Environmental and Energy Study Institute: http://www.eesi.org/fact-sheet-carbon-pricing-around-world-17-oct-2012

Freeman, R. E. (1984). *Strategic management: A stakeholder approach.* New York, NY: HarperCollins.

Friends of the Earth. (2005). *Briefing: Corporate accountability.* Retrieved December 25, 2012, from: www.foe.co.uk/resource/briefings/corporate_accountability1.pdf

Global Reporting Initiative. (n.d.). *Sustainability reporting guidelines.* Retrieved January 11, 2013, from: https://www.globalreporting.org

Goldberg, R. A., & Yagan, J. D. (2007). *McDonald's Corp.: Managing a sustainable supply chain* (Case No. 9-907-414). Cambridge, MA: HBS Premier Case Collection.

Graham, J. (2004). *The perils of the precautionary principle: Lessons from the American and European experience* (Heritage Lectures, No. 818). Retrieved on March 3, 2013, from http://www.heritage.org/Research/Lecture/The-Perils-of-the-Precautionary-Principle-Lessons-from-the-American-and-European-Experience.

Habermas, J. (1985). *The theory of communicative action* (Vol. 2). Boston, MA: Beacon Press.

Hall, D. and Lobina, E. (2009). *The private sector in water in 2009*. Public Sector International Research Unit. Retrieved March 9, 2013, from: http://www.acquabenecomune.org/IMG/pdf/The_private_sector_in_water_in_2009_-David_Hall_-Emanuele_Lobina-Greenwich_University.pdf

Hoffman, A. (2010a). *Molten metal technology (A)* (Case 1-429-049). Ann Arbor, MI: Global Lens.

Hoffman, A. (2010b). *Molten metal technology (B)* (Case 1-429-051). Ann Arbor, MI: Global Lens.

Hub, H. (2012). *Crude oil to natural gas spot price ratio*. Retrieved March 3, 2013, from: http://www.eia.gov/todayinenergy/detail.cfm?id=5830

Huesemann, M., & Huesemann, J. (2011). *Technofix: Why technology won't save us or the environment*. Gabriola Island, Canada: New Society Publishers.

IHS CERA. (2012). *America's new energy future: The unconventional oil and gas revolution and the US economy*. Retrieved on March 3, 2013, from: http://www.ihs.com/info/ecc/a/americas-new-energy-future.aspx

International Telecommunications Union. (2013). *Mobile subscriptions near the 7-billion mark: Does almost everyone have a phone?* Retrieved June 24, 2013 from ITU News: https://itunews.itu.int/En/3741-Mobile-subscriptions-near-the-78209billion-markbrDoes-almost-everyone-have-a-phone.note.aspx

The Johnson Foundation. (2012). *Charting new waters: Financing sustainable water infrastructure*. Retrieved March 9, 2013, from: http://www.johnsonfdn.org/sites/default/files/reports_publications/WaterInfrastructure.pdf

Kolk, A. (1999). Evaluating corporate environmental reporting. *Business Strategy and the Environment 8*(4), 225–237.

Kuuskraa, V., Stevens, S., Leeuwen, T. Van., & Moodhe, K. (2011, April). *World shale gas resources: An initial assessment of 14 regions outside the United States*. Arlington, VA: Advanced Resources International, Inc.

Lane, H. W., Maznevski, M., & Mendenhall, M. (2004). Globalization: Hercules meets Buddha. In H. W. Lane, M. Maznevski, M. E. Mendenhall, & J. McNett (Eds.), *The Blackwell handbook of global management: A guide to managing complexity* (pp. 3–25). Malden, MA: Blackwell Publishers.

Larson, A., & Teichman, W. (2009). *Frito-Lay North America: The making of a net zero snack chip* (UVA-ENT-0112). Charlottesville, VA: Darden School of Business.

Laszlo, C., Christensen, K., Fogel, D., Wagner, G., & Whitehouse, P. (2010). *Berkshire encyclopedia of sustainability, Volume 2: The business of sustainability.* Great Barrington, MA: Berkshire Publishing Group.

Lee, D., & Bony, L. (2007). *Cradle to cradle design at Herman Miller: Moving toward environmental sustainability* (Case No. 9-607-003). Cambridge, MA: HBS Premier Case Collection.

Lemonich, M. D. (2009). Top ten myths about sustainability. *Scientific American Earth 3.0. 19*(1), 40–45.

McDonough, W., & Braungart, M. (2002). *Cradle to cradle: Remaking the way we make things.* New York, NY: North Point Press.

McDonough, W., & Braungart, M. (2013). *The upcycle: Beyond sustainability—Designing for abundance.* New York, NY: North Point Press.

McMaster, J., & Nowak, J. (2009). *Fiji water and corporate social responsibility: Green makeover or "greenwashing"* (Case No. 9B09A008). London, ON: Richard Ivey School of Business Foundation.

McNett, J., & Whitfield, R. (2013*). Metropolitan Water Supply Authority: Evaluating Security Risks.* (Case No. 9B12D025). London, ON: Richard Ivey School of Business Foundation.

Millennium Ecosystem Assessment. (2005). *Ecosystems and human well-being: Biodiversity synthesis.* Washington, DC: World Resources Institute. Retrieved February 14, 2013, from: http://www.scribd.com/doc/5250332/MILLENNIUM-ECOSYSTEM-ASSESSMENT-2005

Mitchell, G. R. (1998). Pedagogical possibilities for argumentative agency in academic debate. *Argumentation & Advocacy 35*(2), 41–60.

Molina, M., & Zaelke, D. (2012, September 25) *A climate success story to build on.* Retrieved on March 3, 2013, from *New York Times*: http://topics.nytimes.com/topics/reference/timestopics/subjects/k/kyoto_protocol/index.html

Morgan, G. M. (2009, December 21). *Why geoengineering?* Retrieved from MIT Technology Review: http://www.technologyreview.com/notebook/416809/why-geoengineering/#comments

National Research Council. (2012). *Induced seismicity potential in energy technologies: Report in brief.* Retrieved on March 3, 2013, from: http://dels.nas.edu/Report/Induced-Seismicity-Potential-Energy-Technologies/13355

Newell, A. (2010). *What is the carbon disclosure project?* Retrieved January 13, 2013, from Triple pundit: People, planet, profit: http://www.triplepundit.com/2010/11/carbon-disclosure-project

Parington, V. L. (1928). Henry thoreau: Transcendental economist. In *Main currents in American thought* (1928 Pulitzer Prize). New York, NY: Harcourt Brace. Retrieved on February 27, 2013, from: http://thoreau.eserver.org/currents.html

Pearce, D., Markandya, A., & Barbieri, E. (2000). *Blueprint for a green economy* (6th ed.). London: Earthscan.

Phills, J., & Denend, L. (2005). *Social entrepreneurs: Correcting market failures (A)* (Case No. S172A). Stanford, CA: Stanford Graduate School of Business.

Pinkham, D. (n.d.). *A guide to corporate transparency.* Retrieved December 12, 2012, from U.S. Public Affairs Council: http://pac.org (Site has limited access as of January 10, 2013.)

Plambeck, E., & Denend, L. (2007). *Wal-Mart's sustainability strategy* (Case No. OIT-71). Stanford, CA: Stanford Graduate School of Business.

Polasky, S. (2008). What's nature done for you lately? Measuring the value of ecosystem services. *Choices: The Magazine of Food, Farm, and Resources Issues 23*(2), 42–46. (Reprinted in *Taking Sides*, pp. 6–11, by R. W. Taylor, 2012, New York, NY: McGraw-Hill)

Porter, M., & Kramer, M. (2011, January). Creating shared value. *Harvard Business Review,* January, Retrieved from http://hbr.org/2011/01/the-big-idea-creating-shared-value

PriceWaterhouseCoopers. (2011). *Shale gas: A renaissance in US manufacturing?* Retrieved March 2, 2013, from OurEnergyPolicy.org: http://www.ourenergypolicy.org/shale-gas-a-renaissance-in-us-manufacturing/

Prinn, R. (2009, December 21). *Why climate scientists support geoengineering research.* Retrieved from MIT Technology Review: http://www.technologyreview.com/video/416870/why-climate-scientists-support-geoengineering-research/

Reinhardt, F., Casadesus-Masanell, R., & Kim, H. (2010). *Patagonia* (Case No. 9-711-020). Boston, MA: Harvard Business School Publishing.

Robock, A., Oman, L., & Stenchikov, G. L. (2008). Regional climate responses to geoengineering with tropical and Arctic SO_2 injections. *Journal of Geophysical Research: Atmospheres 113*(D16), 1984–2012.

Savitz, A. (2006). *The triple bottom line: How today's best-run companies are achieving economic, social and environmental success—and how you can too.* San Francisco, CA: Jossey-Bass.

Schramm, E. (2011). What is flowback, and how does it differ from produced water? Retrieved March 3, 2013, from Institute for Energy and Environmental Research of Northeastern Pennsylvania Clearinghouse: http:energy.wilkes.edu/205.asp

Sher, A. (2012, October 16). *12.72% water rate hike approved for Tennessee American Water customers.* Retrieved March 9, 2013, from Times Free Press.com: http://www.timesfreepress.com/news/2012/oct/16/chattanooga-water-rate-hike-approved/

Spital, F., & Wesley, D. (2010). *Launch of the ford fiesta diesel: The world's most efficient car* (Case No. 9B10M040). London, ON: Richard Ivey School of Business Foundation.

Taylor, S. (2006). *The triple bottom line.* Retrieved December 6, 2012, from University of Texas Austin: www.utexas.edu/features/2006/social/index.html

Thomas, R., Lane, H., & Maznevski, M. (2008). Forensics as a tool for developing global mindsets. Unpublished MS. Copy available on request from R. Whitfield or J. McNett.

Tilmes, S., Müller, R., & Salawitch, R. (2008). The sensitivity of polar ozone depletion to proposed geoengineering schemes. *Science 320*(5880), 1201–1204.

Trick, C. G., Bill, B. D., Cochlan, W. P., Wells, M. L., Trainer, V. L., & Pickell, L. D. (2010). Iron enrichment stimulates toxic diatom production in high-nitrate, low-chlorophyll areas. *Proceedings of the National Academy of Sciences of the United States of America 107*(13), 5887–5892.

Tversky, A., & Kahneman, D. (1974). Judgment under uncertainty: Heuristics and biases. *Science*, New Series *185*(Report Number: 4157), 1124–1131.

United Nations Environmental Programme. (1992). *Rio declaration on environment and development*. Retrieved May 28, 2013, from: http://www.unep.org/documents.multilingual/default.asp?documentid=78&articleid=1163

United Nations Global Compact. (n.d.). *Overview of the UN Global Compact*. Retrieved January 13, 2013, from: http://www.unglobalcompact.org/AboutTheGC/index.html

U.S. Department of Energy. (2011, April). *World shale gas resources: An initial assessment of 14 regions outside the United States*. Retrieved March 2, 2013, http://www.eia.gov/analysis/studies/worldshalegas/pdf/fullreport.pdf

U.S. Geological Survey, U.S. Department of the Interior. (n.d.). *What is sustainability?* Retrieved May 20, 2012, from: http://acwi.gov/swrr/whatis-sustainability-wide.pdf

U.S. Government Accountability Office. (2002). *Water infrastructure: Information on financing, capital planning, and privatization*. Retrieved March 9, 2013, from: http://www.gao.gov/new.items/d02764.pdf

Van Hattum, R. (2006). *Waste = Food*. Icarus Films. Retrieved from: http://icarusfilms.com/new2007/waste.html

Vietor, R., & Reinhardt, F. (1995). *Du Pont Freon® Products Division (A)* (Case No. 9-389-111 Rev: March 28, 1995). Boston, MA: Harvard Business School Publishing

Wackernagel, M., & Rees, W. (1996). *Our ecological footprint: Reducing human impact on the earth*. Gabriola Island, BC, Canada: New Society Publishers.

Water Footprint Network. (n.d.). *Water footprint: Product water footprints— Soft drinks*. Retrieved January 1, 2013 from: http://www.waterfootprint.org/?page=files/Softdrinks

Walthieu, L., & Winig, L. (2007). *Burt's Bees: Leaving the Hive* (Case No. 9-507-017). Boston, MA: Harvard Business School Publishing.

Wells, J., & Haglock, T. (2008). *Whole Foods Market, Inc.* (Case No. 9-705-476 Rev: April 3, 2008). Boston, MA: Harvard Business School Publishing.

Welch, J. B., & Venkateswaran, A. (2009, June). The dual sustainability of wind energy. *Renewable and Sustainable Energy Reviews 13*(5), 1121–1126.

White, G. (2009). *Sustainability reporting: Managing for wealth and corporate health.* New York, NY: Business Expert Press.

Wingspread Conference on the Precautionary Principle. (1998, January 26). Retrieved March 3, 2013, from Science and Environmental Health Network: http://www.sehn.org/wing.html

World Bank. (2007). *Cost of pollution in China: Economic estimates of physical damage.* Washington, DC: The World Bank.

World population prospects: The 2010 revision. (2011). Retrieved March 3, 2013, from United Nations Department of Economic and Social Affairs: http://esa. un.org/wpp/Documentation/pdf/WPP2010_Highlights.pdf

Worstall, T. (2012, July 19). *The cheap way to deal with climate change: Iron fertilisation of the oceans.* Retrieved from Forbes.com: http://www.forbes.com/ sites/timworstall/2012/07/19/the-cheap-way-to-deal-with-climate-change-iron-fertilisation-of-the-oceans/

Wright, I. A., Kemp, S., & Williams, I. (2011). Carbon footprinting: Toward a universally accepted definition. *Carbon Management 2*(1), 61–72.

Yergin, D. (2012, June 10). "America's New Energy Reality." New York Times Sunday Review. Retrieved on October 2, 2013, from http://www. nytimes.com/2012/06/10/opinion/sunday/the-new-politics-of-energy. html?pagewanted=all&_r=0

Index

OTHER TITLES IN OUR ENVIRONMENTAL AND SOCIAL SUSTAINABILITY FOR BUSINESS ADVANTAGE COLLECTION

Chris Laszlo, Case Weatherhead School Of Management
And Robert Sroufe, Duquesne University

- *Strategy Making in Nonprofit Organizations: A Model and Case Studies* by Jyoti Bachani

ALSO IN FORTHCOMING IN THIS COLLECTION

- *IT Sustainability for Business Advantage* by Brian Moore
- *Applying Systems Thinking to Understanding Sustainable Business* by Kerul Kassel
- *Change Management for Sustainability* by Houng Ha

Announcing the Business Expert Press Digital Library

*Concise E-books Business Students Need
for Classroom and Research*

This book can also be purchased in an e-book collection by your library as
- a one-time purchase,
- that is owned forever,
- allows for simultaneous readers,
- has no restrictions on printing, and
- can be downloaded as PDFs from within the library community.

Our digital library collections are a great solution to beat the rising cost of textbooks. e-books can be loaded into their course management systems or onto student's e-book readers.

The **Business Expert Press** digital libraries are very affordable, with no obligation to buy in future years. For more information, please visit **www.businessexpertpress.com/librarians**. To set up a trial in the United States, please contact **Adam Chesler** at *adam.chesler@ businessexpertpress.com* for all other regions, contact **Nicole Lee** at *nicole.lee@igroupnet.com*.

CPSIA information can be obtained
at www.ICGtesting.com
Printed in the USA
BVHW05s1341090718
520941BV00003B/7/P

9 781606 496343